Better Homes and Gardens®

water gardens

written by Eleanore Lewis

Better Homes and Gardens®
Des Moines, Iowa

Better Homes and Gardens® Books
An imprint of Meredith® Books

Water Gardens
Writer: Eleanore Lewis
Project Editor: Cathy Wilkinson Barash
Art Director: Lyne Neymeyer
Copy Chief: Catherine Hamrick
Copy and Production Editor: Terri Fredrickson
Book Production Managers: Pam Kvitne, Marjorie J. Schenkelberg
Contributing Copy Editor: Jay Lamar
Contributing Graphic Designer: Beth Ann Edwards
Contributing Proofreaders: Victoria Beliveau, Tamara Rood, Ellie Sweeney
Contributing Photographers: Ernest Braun, C. Colston Burrell, David Cavagnaro, Crandall and Crandall, Rosalind Creasy, Charles Cresson, Bill Holt, Dency Kane, Brian E. McCay, Charles Mann, Anne Meyer, Stephen Pategas, Roger Sherry, Charles Thomas, Saba S. Tien
Illustrator: Thomas Rosborough
Indexer: Janel Leatherman
Researcher: Rosemary Kautzky
Electronic Production Coordinator: Paula Forest
Editorial and Design Assistants: Kaye Chabot, Mary Lee Gavin, Karen Schirm

Meredith® Books
Editor in Chief: James D. Blume
Design Director: Matt Strelecki
Managing Editor: Gregory H. Kayko

Director, Retail Sales and Marketing: Terry Unsworth
Director, Sales, Special Markets: Rita McMullen
Director, Sales, Premiums: Michael A. Peterson
Director, Sales, Retail: Tom Wierzbicki
Director, Sales, Home & Garden Centers: Ray Wolf
Director, Book Marketing: Brad Elmitt
Director, Operations: George A. Susral
Director, Production: Douglas M. Johnston

Vice President, General Manager: Jamie L. Martin

Better Homes and Gardens® Magazine
Editor in Chief: Jean LemMon
Executive Garden Editor: Mark Kane

Meredith Publishing Group
President, Publishing Group: Christopher M. Little
Vice President, Finance & Administration: Max Runciman

Meredith Corporation
Chairman and Chief Executive Officer: William T. Kerr

Chairman of the Executive Committee: E. T. Meredith III

All of us at Better Homes and Gardens® Books are dedicated to providing you with information and ideas to enhance your home and garden. We welcome your comments and suggestions. Write to us at: Better Homes and Gardens Books, Garden Editorial Department, 1716 Locust St., Des Moines, IA 50309-3023.

If you would like to purchase any of our books, check wherever quality books are sold. Visit our website at bhg.com or bhgbooks.com.

water gardens

introduction

enter the world of water gardening

Imagine. You walk out into your yard, stroll over to a small body of water, and watch bright goldfish darting beneath the spreading leaves of jewel-toned water lilies and among blue-flowered pickerel rush and iris. Hear the friendly "ribbet" of frogs and the lilting song of chickadees. Watch dragonflies glide over the surface of the water, where reflections of blue sky fill patches you left unplanted. Perhaps you listen to the gentle splash of a waterfall or fountain as you sit and admire this little ecosystem you created.

A dream? Not at all. Anyone can build a water garden—just about anywhere. Really. All you need to do is look through the pages of this book, where you will find all kinds of gardens—from tabletop and half-barrel versions to full-size free-form and concrete designs. You will also see accessories such as fountains (you don't even need a pond for some), streams, stepping-stones, a birdbath, and decorative ornaments. You can approach the projects with confidence, too, because we have put together step-by-step directions with information about the expertise and materials the projects require.

the plants

The focus of any water garden, of course, is the plants, and we have gathered a gallery of more than 100 of the best for a variety of pond sizes and sites: water lilies, both hardy and tropical; marginal plants, which, after you pot them up as you would any container plant, you place the pot in water you plant basically as you would any container plants, except that after you pot them you sink them in the water; floating plants, which shade the pond's surface and help prevent algae growth; and edging and companion plants, which you set around the perimeter of a pond to integrate it with your surrounding gardens.

where to begin

Think about where a pond would look good in your yard, and remember that you may want to be able to see it from the house, deck, or patio. Build it next to or as part of an existing garden. Make it a destination at the end of a winding path or a pseudo-stream (You will find directions here for creating a dry creek, if you don't want to go all out with one filled with recirculating water.)

You may think you should start small, but be forewarned: Water gardening is definitely addictive. One water lily will seldom do when three or four would be so much more colorful and eye-catching! And there are so many other plants to discover.

Begin here with a bit of the history of water gardens; then keep reading to see the beauty and delights you can create now.

introduction

from ancient times...

Water, the basis of life, has played a pivotal role in every culture from the dawn of civilization. In fact, what we think of today as water gardening has been a part of civilization for thousands of years.

Early people collected water in holes and canals for crop irrigation. For the ancient Egyptians, water was ornamental as well as useful. They idealized the sacred lotus and water lily on frescoes and tombs. During the golden ages of Greece and Rome, private gardens contained pools decorated with fountains, statues, and plants. Later, in Moorish Spain, water gardens came to the forefront as places for contemplation and appreciation of nature as part of the Islamic vision of paradise that included vast networks of canals and ponds.

From the floating gardens of Mexico and the ancient lakes of the Orient to the enclosed monastic gardens of the Middle Ages, water gardens flourished. Even in the arts, water gardening has left its mark–most notably in the water lilies series of Claude Monet. When you create a water garden you are participating in a venerable tradition.

to the present

The tradition has changed for the better. Thanks to the invention of concrete near the end of the 19th century and the introduction of flexible plastic liners in the 1960s, water gardening is now within the reach of home gardeners.

Couple those advances with the continued cultivation and hybridizing of water lilies, which began in the mid-19th century with the phenomenal work of hybridizer Joseph Latour-Marliac in France and continued into the 20th century with the work of George Pring, among others, in the United States. By working with both hardy and tropical species, .Latour-Marliac gave us many of the brightly colored water lilies we still enjoy.

a spanish garden

right: The palace at Granada, Spain, was built in the 13th century as a summer residence; it overlooks the city and has spectacular views of the distant hills. Water is the dominant feature of the gardens: The Court of the Canal, centerpiece of the gardens, offers still and moving water, light and shadow alternating within a space defined by close plantings.

a stately garden

above: Pergolas and an open summer house provide the backdrop for the large water garden at Old Westbury Gardens on Long Island, New York. Designed in the early 1900s, the estate contains pools filled with lotuses and water lilies, cherub fountains, and statues.

water gardens for all

The exquisite blooms and amazing leaves of water lilies and other water plants have universal appeal. Contrary to popular belief, building and tending the pond they float in isn't difficult at all. The ponds, streams, and container gardens we show you how to create are rated for experience and the length of time it takes to complete the project, so you can select one that you're comfortable with.

consider your time and space

There is a water garden for everyone. You can create one whether you have a large property or a pocket-size yard next to a townhouse. Except for spring and fall cleanup, all you need is an hour each week to take care of a water garden. The rest of the time you can spend simply enjoying it.

container

above: The easiest water garden to make is one you plant in a container, whether you use a stone, plastic, ceramic pot, or a wooden half-barrel. Starting with a small garden—containing one or two plants—helps ensure your success.

preformed pond

left: The beauty of water gardens belies their simplicity. Despite this garden's lush look, anyone can create it in a weekend using a rigid plastic liner, paving stones, and some mature plants.

water gardens | **9**

get ready to garden

You may start out with a rather small water garden, but after a year or two you will probably want to branch out to build a waterfall or a recirculating stream that empties into your soon-to-be-larger pond. A stream is a good means of bridging the gap between two small ponds, making them look as if they were one grand space. A real bridge is another way to camouflage the break between two ponds. Ponds with preformed liners, which are relatively small to begin with, can be easily enlarged that way.

fountain

below right: One of the easiest projects you can do is putting a fountain in a pool or garden bed. The splashing sound of water adds another dimension to a garden, which you can enjoy with or without a pond. Recirculating pumps do seemingly magical feats with water.

lined pond

below: A great invention—the flexible liner—puts water gardening within everyone's building ability. It lets you create any shape you desire. Let your imagination soar.

raised pond

right: Constructing an above-ground pond takes more experience than building one in the ground, but you can achieve some special effects whether you use concrete and stone or wood. Concrete ponds have a long history, and they can last for decades. Wood ponds look good next to decks. The options for size, shape, and location of raised ponds are numerous.

waterfall

left: Recirculating pumps also play a role when you design a waterfall—something best done as you are planning the layout of your pond. A waterfall can be a mere trickle spilling from a single flat, raised stone, or a wash of water pouring down a manufactured incline—and bringing with it enough sound to create an oasis of peace and quiet even in a busy neighborhood.

stream

left: Whether you want a real stream, shown here, or a dry creek that mimics the real thing and only has water in it after a heavy rain, the construction principles are practically the same. Site a stream so that it empties into a pond. In addition, lay hose to recirculate the water. A dry creek, on the other hand, can border the perimeter of your yard without emptying into anything.

the gardens

container gardens: tabletop

zones	time	skill
3–11	2 hours	easy

you will need

- container as desired
- floating plants
- miniature water lily or other plants
- garden soil or aquatic potting mix
- pea gravel

the simplest of water gardens

Dip into water gardening in a small way by setting up a tabletop design. You can use many of the same plants you would in a larger garden; in fact, some that become invasive in a pond behave better in the restricted space of a container.

Choose any container that does not have drainage holes in the bottom. Use floating plants in water. Or treat the plants as if they were marginal or bog plants, and plant them in a layer of soil topped with a layer of pea gravel. Then fill the container with water.

plants for tabletop gardens

floating fern, page 108

miniature water lily, page 120

parrot feather, page 114

water fern, page 109

water lettuce, page 116

water snowflake, page 115

empty containers
right: Containers you can use for a tabletop pond include glazed clay, stone, and glass.

miniature delights

opposite page: For a trailing effect, plant parrot feather to one side. Add water fern with water lettuce.

left: Turn a terra-cotta pot into an exquisite tiny garden by planting a miniature water lily in about 3 to 4 inches of heavy garden soil or aquatic potting mix. Add water to within ½ inch of the rim.

floating paradise

left: Water lettuce and white-flowered water snowflake thrive in a container set on a patio table. You can enjoy a miniature garden indoors as well. Although most water plants will not flower in the subdued light of indoor rooms, the sculptural quality of their leaves often provides enough interest to take the place of blooms. Combine plants that have variegated leaves with those that sport vertical foliage, such as dwarf cattails and papyrus, to create pleasing minigardens.

water gardens | **15**

zones	time	skill
4–10	2 hours	easy

you will need

10"–14" diameter ceramic or stone pot

1–2 tablespoons crushed charcoal (aquarium type)

pebbles or river stones (optional)

floating plants

eye-level beauty

Potted water gardens accent a perennial border or bed, become a focal point in a planting of herbs, or brighten a lightly shaded location.

Creating a potted water garden is easy. Any container (except metal, which can heat the water in summer) will do, as long as it does not have any drainage holes at the bottom. The delight of having the plants at eye level more than makes up for the increased care, which includes keeping a watchful eye on the water level.

If you'd like to include oxygenating plants or fish, you'll need a

container that's at least 12 inches deep. To keep the water fresh and clear, add the crushed charcoal, top with a layer of pebbles or river stones, and fill the pot with water.

Floaters are the easiest water garden plants to use, since they don't require potting. Simply spread out or untangle the roots and set the plants on water.

seasonal care

Check and top off the water level periodically, especially during the hot days of summer.

When cool fall weather arrives with temperatures in the low 50s, move the plants–or the entire container–indoors for the winter.

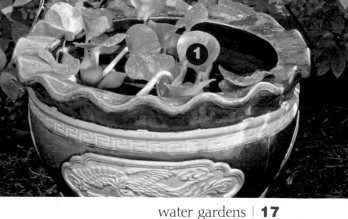

plants

1 water hyacinth, page 110

plant alternatives

water poppy, page 111

water fern, page 109

duckweed, page 113

zones	time	skill
3–11	1 day	easy

you will need

- half whiskey barrel
- flexible or rigid plastic liner
- bricks or cinder blocks
- potted plants
- 3–4 goldfish (optional)

barrels of plants

Whiskey barrels lend themselves to all kinds of plantings, and water gardens are no exception. Their size accommodates several plants as well as a few goldfish and snails.

setting up

Whiskey barrels are watertight as long as they are wet, but to be safe–and to prevent toxins from leaching into the water–line the barrel with a sheet of PVC or EPDM plastic, or a rigid plastic liner (available at nurseries and garden centers). Staple the liner about 2 to 3 inches below the rim, where it won't show.

leveling the pot

Any water garden should be level, whether it is buried in the ground or sitting on a patio. With a container garden, check the level after you have moved it to its permanent place, but before you fill it with water. (Water is incredibly heavy.) If the pot is tilted, move it around on the floor or ground to see if it straightens out; if not, level it with wood shims stuck underneath.

plants

1 hardy water canna, page 118

2 dwarf papyrus, page 110

3 variegated sweet flag, page 108

4 parrot feather, page 114

5 caladium, page 108

6 tropical water lily, page 121

Plant all the plants in garden soil in plastic pots. You can float the floating plants or pot them as well. Placing the floaters on top of the water is the simplest way to maintain them; if they grow too vigorously, remove some from the barrel.

Set the plants in the barrel, placing them on bricks or prewashed cinder blocks to bring them to the correct depth under the water's surface. (See individual entries in Recommended Plants section for the preferred depths.)

fishy business

A whiskey barrel can support three or four small fish—ordinary goldfish. Exotic fish, such as koi, need a larger pond to survive. A location with some shade, particularly at midday, will help the fish survive in water that is often subject to sudden and extreme changes in temperature. In colder zones (below Zone 6), bring the fish indoors to an aquarium for winter.

container gardens: cement pot

zones	time	skill
3–11	3 hours	easy

you will need

- 12"–16" diameter container
- garden soil
- crushed charcoal
- sand or pea gravel
- bricks or cinder blocks
- water plants

the sound of water

Plant containers such as this one following the directions for the whiskey barrel (see page 18). Do not use small pots like these for fish. When winter approaches, bring the plants indoors to a cool, frost-free location. If you leave the container outdoors, empty it of water and clean it.

plants

1 dwarf papyrus, page 110

2 elephant's ear, page 109

3 water fringe, page 115

1 soil To pot a water plant, fill a plastic pot with heavy garden soil. Avoid commercial potting mixes because they contain additives that might separate and float out into the water. Hollow out a planting hole in the center with your hands.

2 placement Set the plant in the hole; untangle and spread out the roots. If the plant has a lot of stems and foliage, cut them back a little to for easier handling while you're potting it. (See page 88 for directions on potting water lilies.)

3 fill Add soil; gently work it and around the roots with your fingers. Tamp the soil firmly but stop short of compacting it. Water the planting thoroughly.

4 mulch Cover the soil with ½" of sand or pea gravel. Water well.. Sink the potted plant into the container or pond, so the rim of the pot sits 4–6 inches below the water's surface. Depending on the depth of the pond, you may need to raise the pot with a brick.

container gardens: plastic pot

zones	time	skill
3–11	1 day	easy

you will need

- 24"–diameter plastic container
- bricks or upturned pots to set potted plants on
- garden soil
- 5–6 tablespoons crushed charcoal (to help maintain water's freshness)
- washed pea gravel
- potted plants
- floating plants

lush planting

When the plants in your water garden begin looking crowded, it is time to divide your plants. You can create more gardens, give the plants away, or even sell some divisions at a local plant sale.

plants

1 chameleon plant, page 111

2 dwarf cattail, page 119

3 four-leaf water clover, page 114

4 hardy water lily, pages 120–125

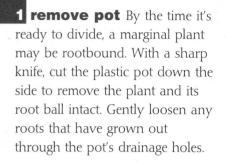

1 remove pot By the time it's ready to divide, a marginal plant may be rootbound. With a sharp knife, cut the plastic pot down the side to remove the plant and its root ball intact. Gently loosen any roots that have grown out through the pot's drainage holes.

2 cut plant Slice through the root ball, cutting it in half. Depending on the size of the plant, you may want to divide it further into fourths or even eighths, but make sure each division has enough roots attached.

3 use a new pot Fill the pot one-fourth to one-half way with fresh garden soil. Center the new division in the pot and fill in around the roots with more soil. Be sure to keep the plant at the same soil depth it was before you divided it.

4 water & mulch Water the plant thoroughly. Cover the soil surface with washed pea gravel or pebbles. Immediately put the plant back in the pond at the same water depth at which it was originally sitting.

edible garden

zones	time	skill
4–11	1 hour	easy

you will need

- plastic pots or tubs
- garden soil
- pea gravel or pebbles
- tubers, corms, plants
- fish emulsion

a tasty garden

A water garden can provide interesting plants to eat as well as beautiful flowers or handsome foliage

You can eat the leaves of water fern, water spinach, and chameleon plant (although some find it too bitter for their taste). The leaves, tuberous roots, and seeds of lotus are mainstays in Asian cuisine. Add the leaves of water celery to soups for a mild celery flavor. Use the leaves of water mint as you would other mints. Harvest the tubers of duck potato and roast them. Watercress, the best known, requires moving water and it difficult to grow successfully in a pot.

right: As you can see, you can plant water chestnuts in any shallow container that will hold water. If you plan to put them in a pond, use a container that has drainage holes in the bottom or sides. Gather the corms of water chestnuts and use them in a stir-fry or hors d'oeuvre.

plants

1 chinese water chestnut, page 110

other edible water plants

chameleon plant	watercress
duck potato	water fern
lotus	water mint
pickerel rush	water spinach
water celery	wild rice

1 plant Start water chestnuts in spring. Put 2–3 inches of soil in an 18-inch container that is at least 6 inches deep. Set the corms 1–2 inches apart. Cover with 1–2 inches of soil. Gently firm the soil. For a pond planting, cover with a layer of pea gravel.

2 water Pour water over the planting to fill the container. Always keep the water level at least 1 inch above the soil. (In a pond or bog, submerge the container so that 4–6 inches of water are above the rim.) Place the plants in full sun. Fertilize every 3 weeks with fish emulsion.

3 harvest Water chestnuts mature in about 6 months. When the foliage turns brown, lift the plants out of the soil. Wash off the soil and rub the foliage off the chestnuts.

4 enjoy To use, peel the chestnuts. Use them in stir fries or wrap with bacon and grill for a crunchy treat. Replant some of the smaller, unpeeled corms in fresh soil for next year's harvest.

sunken container

zones	time	skill
5–10	1 day	easy

you will need

- shovel
- plastic planter
- sand or gravel
- flat stones or flagstones
- marginal plants
- floating plants

mini water garden

Insulate your garden against temperature changes by sinking a pot in the ground rather than on top of the soil so that the surrounding soil insulates it against temperature fluctuations. The minipond also looks particularly attractive at the edge of a path or when surrounded by other plants.

plants

1 dwarf papyrus, page 110

2 water fringe, page 115

3 hardy water canna, page 118

4 duckweed, page 113

5 water snowflake, page 115

1 dig hole Using the pot as a guide, dig a hole slightly larger and deeper than the pot, so the rim sits flush with the surface of the ground. Level the bottom of the hole. Add a layer of sand or gravel if necessary.

2 place pot Set the container in the hole and fill in around it with sand, gravel, or excavated soil to make sure the pot is secure in the hole. (Find a use elsewhere in the garden for the unused excavated soil.)

3 plant Fill the pot with water and let it stand for several days before planting with one water lily, small lotus (*left*), or three to five small potted and floating water plants. You can camouflage the pot with flat stones.

use a horse trough

Almost anything can be used for a water garden. Turn an old or new metal trough–horse, cattle, or pig (available at antiques stores or at animal supply stores)–into a water feature simply by sinking it in the ground; follow the directions for a smaller container (*left*). Add one or two medium-size rocks to connect it visually to the surrounding garden. Camouflage the rim with a covering of rocks and flat stones, or leave it in view, accented with plantings. Put a fountain near one end.

millstone fountain

zones	time	skill
4–9	3 days	easy

you will need

- 5' diameter 18" deep plastic tub
- pump and fountain jet
- shovel
- 3'–4' length of pressure–treated 1×4 board
- sand or gravel
- 4' diameter millstone or other large, flat stone
- decorative stones

the sound of water

A spray of water adds immeasurably to any yard or garden. You can create such an ornament with a millstone or grindstone. Or, drill a hole in the center of a flat stone or slab of concrete.

plants

1 siberian iris, page 112

2 fern, page 127

3 hosta 'Elegans', page 127

4 hosta 'Francee', page 127

5 horsetail, page 111

6 hosta, page 127

use a large bowl

A large ceramic bowl is a stylish alternative to a millstone fountain. Carefully drill a hole through the bottom of the bowl. You can adjust the height of the fountain from a low level that barely breaks the surface to a spurt of water that shoots into the air. If you live in an area with freezing winters, drain the fountain and bring the bowl inside for the winter to prevent breaking or cracking. Bowls of different colors will give different effects.

millstone fountain

1   **base** Use a shallow whiskey-barrel liner that is slightly larger in diameter than the largest millstone or the grindstone and deep enough for you to submerge the pump. The water from the pump will spill over the stone into the liner, and the pump will recirculate it. Choose a location near a GFCI electrical source, whether in a garden bed, alongside a patio, or near a walkway. Dig a hole deep enough to set the liner in flush with the ground, and slightly wider than the liner.

2   **level** Set the liner in the hole, making sure it is level. If it isn't, lift out the liner and spread sand, gravel, or some of the excavated soil in the bottom of the hole to create a level surface. Replace the liner in the hole and add soil around its sides to hold it in place. Remove any soil you accidentally get in the liner.

3   **pump** Place the water pump in the center of the liner. This project requires only gentle water pressure; choose the smallest one available. Arrange river rocks or pieces of chipped brick under the pump to lift it nearly level with the top of the liner. Make sure it is secure by surrounding it with more rocks or chipped brick.

support Lay a board (either pressure-treated, cedar, or redwood to prevent rotting) across the top of the liner and mark the spot where the board matches up with the pump. Cut a hole at that spot large enough for the pump spray to bubble through. Notch the ends of the board so it will sit securely on the liner. Put the board back on the liner. The board will distribute the weight of the stones and leave the liner unharmed.

4

millstone With help from an assistant, position the millstone(s) over the board, matching the holes with the hole in the board and with the pump. Gently lower the stones. Fill the liner with water.

5

finish Connect the pump to the electrical source. Adjust the water flow as desired; use a flow restricter if necessary. Conceal the ends of the board and the rim of the liner with mulch, rock, or spreading plants. Keeping soil out of the liner will keep the water clean. Even though the pump will recirculate the water, add more periodically to offset evaporation, especially during hot summer days. If you live in an area where winter temperatures regularly drop below freezing, remove the pump before the first fall freeze; reposition it the following spring.

6

raised ponds: preformed liner

zones	time	skill
4–10	2 days	moderate–experienced

why build one?

There are a number of reasons to build a raised pond rather than set one in the ground. First and foremost are the aesthetics–the view. A raised pond is closer to eye level, so you can enjoy it when you sit on the cap or nearby on a deck or patio.

Secondly, it's easy to maintain. You don't need to bend over far to care for the plants or to clean the surface. Finally, there is the ground itself: Your soil may be too moist (strange as that may sound when talking about a pond), or it may be too rocky to dig out a level area.

plants

1 hardy water lily, pages 120–125

2 tropical water lily, pages 120–125

annuals for color

a yellow culinary sage

b globe amaranth

c purple culinary sage

d begonia

raised ponds: preformed liner

1   **day one:** Build the raised wood pond on a level surface so that the framing will be square. For the 82"×49" base, nail together a frame with two long and two of the shorter 2×4s, using simple butt joints. Mark the short sides one-third in from each end and nail the remaining two 2×4s in as supports. Nail the pressure-treated plywood on top. Then build the side panels with the redwood 2×2s; space the 2×2 uprights about every 12 inches and nail them in. Reinforce the corners by adding a 2×2 upright 2" from each corner. Make the end panels with 2×4s for the corner uprights and 2×2s for the top and bottom rails; add 2 spaced 2×2 uprights to each end panel. Finally, nail side and end panels onto the base, butting and nailing the corners together.

2   Cut the 2-inch-thick piece of plastic-foam insulation to fit inside the framework and set it down on the base. Lay the CDX unfinished plywood on top of the insulation. Put the pond liner inside the frame, resting the liner lip on the 2×2 top rail.

3   Butt and nail 1×4 cedar trim at the corners, using one straight piece and one ripped piece for each corner. Cut the cedar lap siding to fit between the trim pieces and nail it in place to the frame uprights; toenail the siding to the corner trim. Leave slightly open at the top on each side.

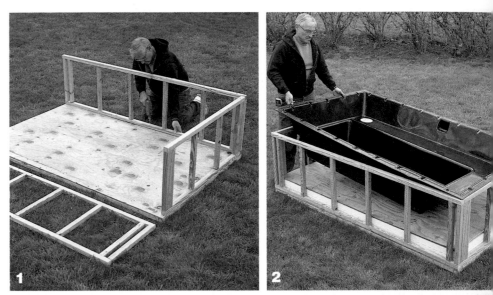

day two: Move the pond to its final location while it's light enough to transport easily. Select a site that is level and has access to an electrical outlet (for pump and filter). When the pond is in place, fill the cavity between the siding and the liner with masonry insulation.

Nail on the top pieces of lap siding. Finish filling the interior cavity with insulation by pouring it in with the help of a dustpan.

Build a cap with mitered corners, using cedar 2×8s; remember to measure the length at the longest point of the miter. Attach the cap to the frame with galvanized screws placed approximately every 12 inches. Add cedar 1×8 trim boards around the entire structure just below the cap to cover gaps; nail them to the frame.

Fill the pond with water and treat to dechlorinate it. (Garden centers and pet stores carry dechlorinating aids.) Add a pump and filter to keep the water oxygenated and clean, a small fountain for aeration and pleasant sound, and a pond heater if you plan to overwinter fish.

Set water lilies and other water plants in the pond. Wait a couple of weeks before adding fish. Dress up the perimeter of the pond with containers of annuals, perennials, and herbs for all-season color.

raised ponds: flexible liner

zones	time	skill
3–10	2 days	moderate

you will need

pressure-treated lumber:
    two 2×2s, 8' long
    seven 2×8s, 8' long
    six 1×2s, 8' long
    two 2×4s, 8' long

deck screws (corrosion-resistant flathead screws): 2", 2½", 3", 3½"

wood shims

flexible liner at least 66" square, 35 mil thick

staple gun, table saw, drill, screwdriver

scissors or utility knife

white stain or exterior latex paint (optional)

pond pump-and-fountain kit (optional)

classic look

Easy to build and right for a small patio. this project is smaller and takes less time than the pond on pages 32 to 35 with the preformed liner This raised pond's flexible liner leaves room for mistakes, that is, less than perfect measuring. If you want to put it on your deck,

remember that it will be quite heavy when filled with water–at least 600 pounds. Be sure the deck can support it.

setting it up

The best plants for a pond this size are miniature water lilies and a single full-size hardy or tropical lily. Wait to buy plants until the pond is finished and filled with water. Use water from a garden hose, then dechlorinate it with one of the many available treatments. Plug in the pump after planting. Wait one to two weeks before adding fish or snails. The pond will accommodate two, possibly three, goldfish; koi need a larger, deeper pond.

plants

1 tropical water lily, pages 120–125

2 water hyacinth, page 110

3 parrot feather, page 114

4 floating fern, page 108

raised ponds: flexible liner

1 **base frame** Refer to the illustration, right, as needed. Cut the 2×2s into 36-inch lengths for the base frame. Assemble the frame with 3-inch deck screws, first drilling countersunk pilot holes for all screws to avoid splitting the lumber.

2 **base** Crosscut three of the 2×8s to make five 36-inch-long pieces. Place them edge to edge. Mark the last board so the overall width of the base is 36 inches; cut all boards to size. Place the base frame on a flat work surface. Center the boards on top, and drive 2½-inch deck screws through the base into the base frame. Take the base and position it where you want the water garden to be.

3 **sides** Crosscut the remaining four 2×8s into 36-inch lengths for the eight side pieces. Assemble them into two boxes, using 3½-inch deck screws. Place one box on the base assembly. Miter the 1×2 banding to run around the perimeter of the box. Center the banding on the joint line between the box sides and the base; fasten it with 2-inch deck screws, driving some screws into the box sides, others into the base.

4 **assemble** Stack the second box on the first. Screw on two more sets of banding: one straddling the joint line, the other flush with the top of the sides. Cut a ½" by ½" notch at one corner for the pump's electrical cord (see notch in illustration 6).

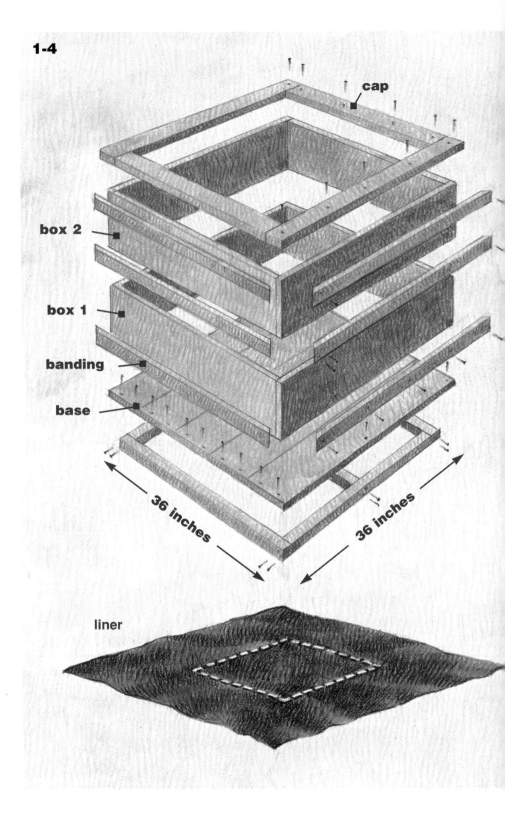

1-4

cap

box 2

box 1

banding

base

36 inches

36 inches

liner

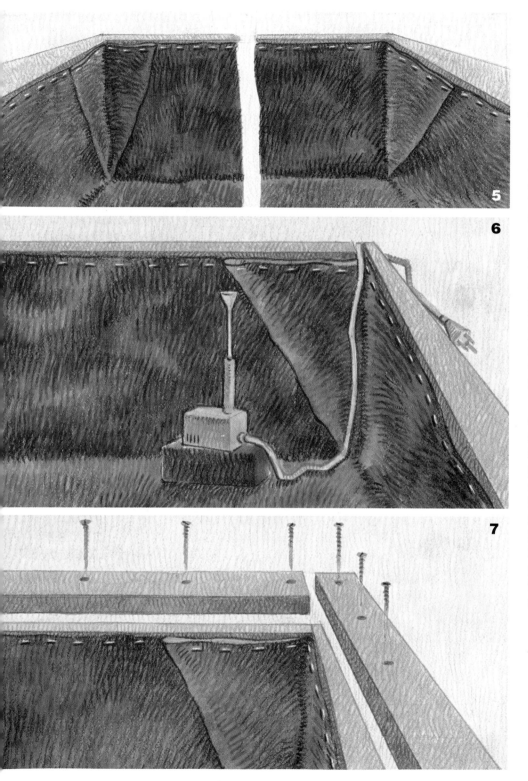

liner Cut the flexible pond liner to **5** a manageable size. A 66-inch square will provide you with a 1½-inch allowance on all sides. Put the liner in the box and roughly center it. Divide the surplus of the liner into equal pleats on each side (left side in illustration) or pleat all of it to one side (right side in illustration). Drive staples through the liner all along the sides near the top. Trim the liner flush with the top of the sides, using heavy scissors or a utility knife.

pump Position the pump where you **6** want it inside the box, centered or off to one side. If you will plant water lilies, place the pump in the corner opposite the plants because they prefer still water. Raise the pump on stacked bricks so the fountain will be above the surface of the water. Guide the electrical cord through the notch you made in Step 4.

cap Crosscut the 2×4 lumber into **7** four cap strips, the lengths indicated in the drawing opposite, and screw them in place with 3-inch deck screws. Double-check the location of the completed box before you fill it with water, making sure it's near a GFCI electrical outlet. When filed, it will weight close to 600 pounds. Level the pond with wood shims if necessary. Paint the outside of the pond, if you want, or let it weather naturally to a soft gray.

concrete pond

zones	time	skill
5–10	8–9 days	difficult

you will need

- garden hose or rope
- shovel
- masonry trowel
- ready–mix concrete
- concrete reinforcing mesh
- 6" stakes
- polyethylene sheets
- bricks, pavers, or cut stone
- pipe or conduit
- stiff bristle brush
- pool paint (optional)

classic pond

Long before preformed and flexible liners came into existence, concrete was the material of choice for ponds. It is inexpensive and long-lasting, if you take

plants

1 cinnamon fern, page 127

2 hardy water lily, pages 120–125

surrounding plants

a candytuft

precautions and some extra care in building and maintaining the concrete.

precautions

A pond with sloping sides is easier to build than one with straight sides. To build a pond with straight sides, you need to add wooden forms to hold the concrete while it begins to cure. Build the pond in mild dry weather so that rain or high temperatures don't interfere with the concrete curing properly.

maintenance

If you live in an area with subfreezing temperatures, you will need to drain the pond for winter to prevent ice from cracking the concrete. Rent a pump for that purpose. Move the plants and fish indoors; put the fish in an unheated aquarium. In zones 9 to 11, you don't need to empty the water or move the fish unless it's time for the pond's annual cleaning.

concrete pond

1   **dig and prepare** Decide on the shape of the pond, using a garden hose or rope. Remember to consider the thickness of the concrete and add about 4 inches all around. Outline the shape with lime or spray paint. Excavate the soil, digging to the depth you want plus 4 inches for the concrete; slope the sides to about a 45-degree angle. Dig a shelf for edge plants, if desired. Compact the earth on the bottom and especially on the sides. Make sure the top edges of the pond are level. (See Step 2 on page 56.) If you include a pump and fountain, decide where to place the electrical cord and water-return line.

2   **reinforce** Contour concrete reinforcing mesh in the hole. About 12 inches above the bottom, drive in 6-inch stakes to hold the mesh. The stakes also will guide you in keeping the concrete a uniform 4 inches thick.

3   **pour** Pour the ready-mix concrete into one part of the pool at a time (concrete sets up quickly) and pack it into the mesh with a trowel. When you reach 4-inch thickness, pull out the stakes or drive them into the ground; fill the stake holes with concrete. Pour the next portion. Dampen the concrete periodically to retard the curing process.

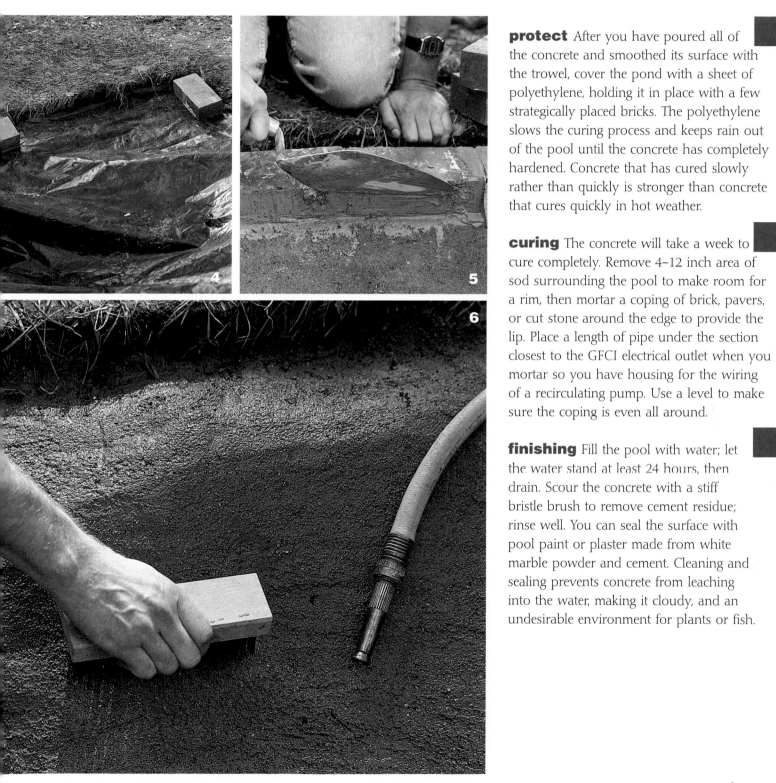

protect After you have poured all of the concrete and smoothed its surface with the trowel, cover the pond with a sheet of polyethylene, holding it in place with a few strategically placed bricks. The polyethylene slows the curing process and keeps rain out of the pool until the concrete has completely hardened. Concrete that has cured slowly rather than quickly is stronger than concrete that cures quickly in hot weather.

4

curing The concrete will take a week to cure completely. Remove 4–12 inch area of sod surrounding the pool to make room for a rim, then mortar a coping of brick, pavers, or cut stone around the edge to provide the lip. Place a length of pipe under the section closest to the GFCI electrical outlet when you mortar so you have housing for the wiring of a recirculating pump. Use a level to make sure the coping is even all around.

5

finishing Fill the pool with water; let the water stand at least 24 hours, then drain. Scour the concrete with a stiff bristle brush to remove cement residue; rinse well. You can seal the surface with pool paint or plaster made from white marble powder and cement. Cleaning and sealing prevents concrete from leaching into the water, making it cloudy, and an undesirable environment for plants or fish.

6

concrete pond

classic style
right: Concrete ponds cover a range of styles, from traditional to naturalistic. This concrete-edged pond, with its gently bubbling fountain, quaint cherub, and lily pads, presents a classic sight.

natural look
below: Pavers hide the waterfall mechanics; the flat-stone edge surround provides a natural look.

reflections

above: The mortarless dry-stack stone wall surrounding this concrete pond matches other walls on the property. Plantings accent the pond's edge, and the water is open to the sky. It reflects trees and shrubs through the changing seasons.

small space

left: Even a small pond will accent a garden or patio. With room for just a few plants and goldfish, this pond brings serenity to a lightly shaded patio. The sturdy, narrow bluestone ledge provides a welcome place to relax and watch the fish in action.

water gardens | **45**

ponds with liners: flexible liner

zones	time	skill
4–11	3–5 days	moderate

you will need

flexible liner, 20–45 mil thick

garden hose or lime; string and stakes

shovel, carpenter's level

2×4 (for leveling)

builder's sand

sheets of newspaper, carpet, or geo-fabric

stones, pavers

pump-and-fountain kit

charming beauty

You have many more options for shapes and sizes when you build a pond with a flexible liner, but it does take planning and some additional building time. Although you can make any shape you

plants

1 lily-of-the-nile, page 126

2 siberian iris, page 112

3 water lettuce, page 116

4 tropical water lily, pages 120–125

5 purple taro, page 109

surrounding plant

a birdsfoot ivy

want, simple shapes are easier to excavate and set up. And, a pond with a flexible liner is much easier to install– and takes less time– than a rigid, preformed pond liner.

site planning

Select a site that is away from deciduous trees, so you aren't constantly cleaning out fallen flowers in spring and leaves in autumn–a wise precaution no matter what material you are using for your water garden. Even though you will pad the ground underneath the pond before laying down the liner, try to avoid rocky areas. Rocks can puncture the liner.

ponds with liners: flexible liner

1 **select a site** Choose a location in direct sun or with midday light shade if you live in warmer zones. Most water plants grow best with at least 6 hours of sun daily.

Don't place the pond at the lowest point in the yard. Water runoff from heavy rains can cause problems.

2 **outline** Decide on the shape of the pond. (Make a preliminary drawing on paper, indicating the pond's relationship to other areas in the yard.) Use a garden hose or lime to outline curved sections. If your design includes straight edges, stretch a length of string between stakes for those sections.

Look at the pond's shape and location from afar–from the patio, the deck, even inside the house–to get a feeling for how the finished project will look. Rearrange the outline until you have a shape you like.

3 **dig** Excavate the hole at least 18 inches deep, preferably with the assistance of a couple of helpers. Slope the sides and keep the bottom flat.

At one end, along one side, or all around the pond, dig a 1-foot-wide terrace 8 to 12 inches deep to hold containers of marginal plants.

If you plan to edge the pond with flat stones or bricks, dig a ledge 3 to 4 inches wide for that purpose.

level Lay a 2×4 across the pond and set
a construction level on it to check that the
edge is the same height all around. Keeping
the edge level will prevent the liner from
showing when you have filled the pond.

4

If the pond is too wide for the 2×4, attach
a line level to a length of string; pull the
string taut at different points across the
length and width of the excavation.

Add or remove soil until the edge is level.
Then lower a small section of the edge by an
inch to allow overflow to drain off during
heavy rains.

underlayment If the soil is very
rocky, spread 2 inches of sand over the
bottom before laying down the
underlayment.

5

Cover the bottom and sides of the
pond with an underlayment of several
layers of newspapers spread in full
sections, old carpet, or geo-fabric to
protect the liner from protruding
rocks and roots.

liner To figure out the liner size you
need, measure the pond length and width,
then add twice the depth plus 2 feet all
around to allow for overlap.

6

Move the liner gently into position in the
excavation. Leave wrinkles for slack along the
curves. Temporarily anchor the edge of the
liner with stones or pieces of lumber.

Slowly fill the pond with water; ease, fold,
and smooth the liner as needed. The wrinkles
will not show when the pond is full.

7 **edging** Remove the stones you used to temporarily hold the liner in place. Set flat stones around the rim of the pond on the 3-inch ledge and secure the edge of the liner under them.

Abut any irregularly shaped stones as if they were pieces of a puzzle. They should form a fairly level first course (layer). Use pavers, bricks, flagstones, or cut stones to build the edge. If you want, position some of the pavers or stones so they overhang the rim of the pond.

8 **trim** Using sharp scissors, trim the liner all around to within 1 foot of the edge of the first course of stones.

9 **second course** Set a second course of stones on top of the first, pulling the liner securely under the stones as you lay them. Center each stone over the joint of a stone in the first course. Double edging ensures that the liner will not slip.

The liner is invisible from the pond side. To hide it on the exterior side, use edging plants. Take your time in deciding on the plants to place around the pond. Good choices to consider are coreopsis, creeping thyme, daylilies, dianthus, fountain grass, hostas, liriope, and sedums.

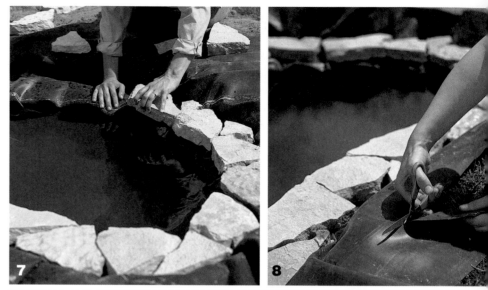

additions If you want, add one or two [10] more courses of stones to create a decorative edging, which will have the appearance of a dry stack stone wall. This raised wall is perfect for holding a larger fountain or a small spitter (decorative object that sprays water into the pond). Plan for that before you place the second course of stones. Leave a small opening through which to guide the tube from the recirculating pump to the fountain.

pump If you include a pump and [11] fountain in the pond, rest it on the bottom of the pond–in the center, off to one side, or near one end. Bring a small pump closer to the surface by putting it on bricks or cinder blocks. (Scrub cinder or concrete blocks with a stiff brush dipped in a solution of 1 part vinegar and 3 parts water, then rinse.) Keep the fountain away from water lilies, which prefer still or nearly still water.

plant Use a dechlorinating product to [12] treat the water. Then set in plants.

Raise plants, such as water lilies, to correct heights by placing the pots on bricks or concrete blocks.

Place marginal plants, such as Japanese iris, papyrus, and cattails, in pots on the terrace created in Step 3.

Wait for a week or two for the water to naturally dechlorinate before adding fish.

ponds with liners: rigid liner

zones	time	skill
4—11	2 days	moderate

you will need

- preformed pond liner
- lime, paint, or rope
- stakes
- shovel
- sand
- pump
- assorted rocks and flat stones
- potted plants
- floating plants

easy design

A pond with a rigid liner is like a large sunken container, with subtle differences. A preformed pond offers more space for plants (diameter and depth) and it takes more time to build. Although you can approximate the exterior shape, you need to be more exact with the length, width, and placement of the interior marginal shelf. Excavating the hole will be easier if you avoid rocky areas and those with large tree roots. Once you've placed the liner, gradually fill in around it with sand.

under cover

Camouflage the rim of the liner by laying rocks and flat stones on it; place some so they overhang the water for a natural look. Accent the pond with a surrounding bed of perennials and annuals. Turn some of the flat stones into shelves holding potted flowering and foliage plants, if you want.

plants

1 hosta, page 127

2 caladium, page 108

3 leucothoe, page 127

4 cattail, page 119

5 fern, page 127

6 duckweed, page 115

7 water hyacinth, page 110

clay pond

zones	time	skill
3–11	3–4 days	experienced

you will need

shovel

bald cypress or other planks: 1" thick × 12" wide; thinner for curved sections

30"–42" long pipes (iron water pipes)

sledgehammer

naturally beautiful

A natural clay-sided pond has several distinct advantages–if you have good clay soil in which to build it. First, the soil can stabilize an eroding bank while it keeps the area as natural as possible–no plastic rims or concrete sides to contend with. You can turn a much-used drainage ditch into an attractive asset rather than an eyesore by emptying it into a clay pond. And if you have an existing natural pond improve it by reinforcing the sides, as shown *opposite*.

a few pointers

Use any lumber for the sides because it won't rot under water. If a nearby stream is the source of water, direct the water from it through a pipe to the pond to avoid any sediment buildup. Close off the pipe in order to drain the pond for cleanup.

plants

1 astilbe, page 126

2 blue flag, page 112

3 cardinal flower, page 113

4 variegated yellow flag, page 112

5 western skunk cabbage, page 113

6 marsh marigold, page 108

7 Japanese primrose, page 116

8 canna, page 109

1 **set planks** Dig out the shape. Lay the planks on edge and hammer the pipes 18 inches into the ground to hold the frame in place; in a section by a slope, stack two planks. For curved sections, soak thinner planks in water overnight to soften, then bend them into a curve. Set them on top of thicker, straight planks.

2 **water** Fill the pond with water; the planks will not show because they will be at least 1 inch below the surface. Even if water seeps out–and it will, despite a packed clay bottom–bog plants should survive. To accommodate water lilies, floating plants, and fish, keep a garden hose handy for topping off the pond.

pond with fountain

zones	time	skill
4–11	2 hours	easy

you will need

- pump and fountain or pump-and-fountain kit
- concrete or cinder blocks or bricks
- outlet with ground fault circuit interrupter

rippling water

Even if you enjoy the simple, peaceful calm of still water, in time you may be unable to resist adding a fountain to your water garden. If you live in a busy suburban or urban neighborhood, you may find a fountain invaluable because it masks the

plants

1. dwarf cattail, page 119
2. hardy water canna, page 118
3. pickerel rush, page 116
4. Siberian iris, page 112
5. hardy water lily, pages 120–125
6. creeping jenny, page 114

surrounding street noises with the sound of running water.

Putting a fountain in your pond is an easy project. So many kinds of fountains are available; you may have a difficult time deciding which one to choose. Let the style of your pond and landscape guide you. (There are gentle bubblers and mushroom–or bell-shape sprays, gushers, upright sprays and jets, fountains that sit on pumps just below the surface of the water, and others that pour water from classical statuary.)

Whatever type you choose, it will need the same basic equipment: a pump, sized according to the size of the pond and the fountain; tubing to connect the pump to the fountain; and a nearby electrical outlet that has a ground fault circuit interrupter.

pond with fountain

hoses

The hose that circulates the water between the pump and the fountain may be black or transparent. Use clamps to make a water-tight seal between the hose ends and the pump and fountain. If you purchase a pump-and-fountain kit, the hose and fixtures will be included. You may need a flow control valve, depending on your water pressure.

raise it up

Most ponds are deeper than 18 inches (the shallowest recommended), and the mechanics of most fountains are relatively small. This is especially true of the small sprays or bubblers that attach directly to a pump. To raise them to the surface, set them on concrete blocks or on bricks.

electricity

Any time you combine electricity and water, you have a potentially dangerous situation. Always connect electrical plugs to outlets that are equipped with a ground fault circuit interrupter (GFCI).

fountain patterns

As noted on page 57, fountains are available in many spray patterns and sizes. Consider the size of your pond to decide which to install.

the pond in winter

Prepare a pond for winter by removing plants that are not hardy. Fish can remain in a pond that is deep enough not to freeze solid, as long as the water surface stays clear of ice. To prevent it from icing over, use a floating or submersible water heater (de-icer) plugged into a GFCI-equipped outlet.

filters

Consider adding a filter to your pond pump to help extend its life and to keep the fountain nozzles clear of debris. (Pump or modular filters are different from pond filters. See mechanicals, pages 94 to 95.)

pond with waterfall

zones	time	skill
4–11	4 days	moderate

you will need

- pond (flexible liner, concrete, or preformed liner)
- submersible pump
- brick or stone
- vinyl tubing
- flat and rough stones
- outlet with ground fault circuit interrupter
- mortar (optional)

running water

The sights and sounds of water splashing into a pond recall images of clear springs and woodland brooks. To turn that into a reality in a backyard water garden, all you need is a recirculating pump, some tubing, and rocks. Plan for the waterfall before you begin building the pond, and install the tubing as you build. As you excavate the pond hole, pile the soil at the end where you want the waterfall to cascade.

Water lilies prefer still or almost-still water, so plant them at a distance from the waterfall. Notice that in the picture, *left*, the water lilies are not affected by the splashing water because they are planted near the opposite side. Fish, on the other hand, don't mind moving water at all.

seasonal concerns

In zones 3 to 7, you will need to disconnect the pump in winter, but you can leave it in the pond. If you have raised it by placing it on a brick or stone, take it off and set it on the bottom of the pond. Empty the water from the tubing.

echo chamber

An echo chamber amplifies the sound of water that falls in front of a recessed wall. To make one, cantilever a large flat stone several inches over the edge of the pond, 6 inches or more above the water. Tuck another flat stone against the side of the pond to form the vertical back of the chamber. Stack rocks about 2 inches high on the cantilevered stone, tilting them slightly toward the water. Run the tube between the rocks.

plants

1 hardy water lily, pages 120-125

2 siberian iris, page 112

3 laevigate iris, page 112

4 dwarf papyrus, page 110

pond with waterfall

coping

Edge the pond with pavers, brick, flagstone, or cut stone. Lay the coping over the exposed liner that extends beyond the pond. Place the stones even with the edge or slightly overhang them. Mortar the pavers in place, if desired.

pump

Pumps for ponds are waterproof and submersible. Raise the pump off the bottom by placing it on a brick or concrete block. Connect the tubing before you fill the pond, but do not plug in the pump until the pond is filled. The height of the waterfall and the size of the pond will determine the appropriate pump size.

water

Fill the pond slowly–after you have built the waterfall and before you mortar the dripstone (an optional step). Plug in the pump and adjust the dripstone until you like the sound of the waterfall.

waterfall

Lay flexible PVC liner from 1 foot below the rim of the pond to the highest level of the stream; hide the liner and keep it in place with rough and flat stones. Set flat stones at the top. Overhang the dripstone above the pond–the distance of the overhang affects the sound of the falling water, so experiment before you mortar it (optional) into place.

recirculate

Use the soil excavated from the pond hole to build a stair-step waterfall. Decide first where it will begin, so you can stretch the vinyl tubing from the pump to the top of the waterfall before sculpting the downhill ridges and pools.

spillway

A spillway is lined with flat stones or pavers, and its descent from source to pond is more gradual than that of a waterfall. Its purpose is to direct water runoff from reservoirs, and it also looks and sounds attractive when it empties recirculated water into a pond. Build it in the same way as the water course, *below;* the ridges should be less pronounced.

pond with waterfall

unique style

above: A waterfall or fountain helps aerate the water, which is good for fish and plants. The aesthetic benefits far outweigh the practicalities. As much sculpture as waterfall, this structure is beautiful in its simplicity. Three concave stones rest on an iron ladder platform; set at a slight angle, each stone pours water onto the stone below. A pump in the pond constantly pushes water up the tubing to the spout.

country charm

right: As rustic as can be, this stone waterfall includes an echo chamber. The design resembles a rock slide with pennywort naturally covering any bare ground leading to the pond below.

stillness

left: Although the waterfall is near water lilies (which prefer still water) the lotus leaves absorb much of the water movement.

rock alternatives

right: A pond just big enough to support a few fish and a water lily is a pleasing destination with the addition of a waterfall. The builder wedged a copper basin into the side of a rockery on a slope and buried the recirculating hose in a narrow passage under the first stratum of rocks.

moisture

below: Sited next to a patio, the small waterfall and tiny pool provide humidity for the houseplants summering along the edge. The waterfall empties from a narrow stream built to run through the garden, which borders a backyard lawn. The falls are one level high—an easy do-it-yourself project.

dry creek

zones	time	skill
3–11	2 days	moderate

you will need

- rope or garden hose
- shovel
- rototiller (optional)
- permeable landscape fabric
- river stones, rough rocks, pebbles
- boulders
- flat stones (stepping stones)

waterless stream

Sometimes all it takes is the impression of a stream. Many people have unused areas in the yard because these spaces do not seem to lend themselves to a pretty garden design. The most common unused spaces include a wet expanse of ground at the rear of the property and another is a side yard. Both places present an opportunity to take advantage of disadvantages.

A dry streambed can function as a drainage ditch for the wet area, while its beauty masks the utilitarian aspect. A well-planted dry creek can filter obtrusive street noises in the side yard. A winding trail of polished or rough stones bordered by hedges and beds of colorful annuals and perennials is very peaceful.

Side yards and rear property lines often include fences, which make excellent backdrops for

plants

1 japanese pittosporum, page 127
2 impatiens, page 127
3 sweet flag, page 108
4 kaffir lily, page 126

plantings. The addition of a dry streambed is a perfect opportunity for designing a special garden retreat.

a few pointers

To save money, put in an underlayment of ordinary rough stones and use polished river stones for the top layer only. The subdued gray color of the river stones, left, beautifully offsets the greens and floral hues of the plants.

Utilize plants that live naturally beside a real stream such as iris, cardinal flower, hostas, and astilbes. Summer some of your houseplants, such as clivia and orchids, outdoors in the shelter of a fenced dry creek garden. They will appreciate the heat reflected from the stones and the shelter from the wind and hot sun.

dry creek

1   **design and dig** Using rope or a garden hose, lay out the contours of the stream in a meandering, casual style. Vary the width. To make digging easier, you can rototill the creek bed first. If the stream is very large, you may want to rent an earthmoving tractor to cut the initial swath. Use the excavated soil to mound a creek bank or to fill low spots elsewhere on your property. Dig the bed to a depth of 6 to 8 inches. Even on flat property, the bed should run slightly downhill, so it can carry water during heavy rains.

2   **shape** It's visually interesting to have some straight, deep sides and some more casual. Shape and smooth the sides and the bottom; they do not need to be perfectly smooth. Remove twigs, roots, stones, and other objects that might puncture the landscape fabric. Remove weeds and plants. Chop through large roots with an ax. Work around main tree roots.

3   **lay fabric** Working on a still day, spread at least two layers of landscape fabric, such as permeable Typar polypropylene fabric. With two layers, your dry creek will last a long time, eliminating the need to remove the covering rock and replace the fabric if it wears out. If you want the creek to carry water, use a solid plastic. Place stones to secure the fabric. Smooth out each layer and overlap the bed edges.

stonescape Select a stone in scale **4** with the size of the stream. Smooth river rocks give the illusion of a more active creek; rough stones give the impression that the creek has been dry for quite a while. Use a depth of 4 inches along the base of the stream; mound the stones 6 to 8 inches deep along the edges to meet the banks. Place stepping-stones, if you want, or add another point of interest, such as a waterfall made with stacked stones.

anchor Use boulders to anchor the **5** landscape fabric that drapes up the sides and over the bank. Fill in with smaller boulders and river rocks to hide the fabric. Add more stones to the creek and up the sides, as desired.

landscape Create a natural look **6** along the edges of the stream, keeping the edges a little rough and irregular. Bury larger stones at least half their height in the soil rather than laying them directly on top of the soil. Soften the edges of the creek with groundcovers and perennials that will spread—most won't be able to find a good place to root in the stream itself. If some do, prune them occasionally to keep them overhanging instead of invading. Plant a few evergreen shrubs and dwarf trees along the creek and in beds nearby. Fashion a stepping-stone bridge or a raised wooden bridge, if you want.

pond with stream

zones	time	skill
4–11	2 days	moderate

you will need

- shovel
- PVC liner
- submersible pump
- tubing
- assorted rough and flat stones, rocks
- paver (bridge, optional)

a natural look

Plantings around a pond connect it to the surrounding landscape, but nothing makes a pool look more natural than a meandering stream. If you are lucky enough to have an existing stream on your property, you can site a pond anywhere along it, or you can divert part of the stream to the ideal location of the pond. No stream? Perhaps you have a drainage ditch at the rear of your property that periodically fills with water, since its purpose is to handle runoff. Instead, create a burbling stream. To make the stream look

natural, camouflage its source with a mixed planting of shrubs and perennials and outcroppings of stone.

building a stream

Basically there are only a few differences between constructing a dry stream-bed and a stream. Use a liner that is not permeable for a stream with flowing water, unlike the semi-permeable liner used in the dry stream-bed (see pages 66 to 69). To recirculate the water, bury the plastic tubing from the pump in the pond along the bank to the stream's source. The distance the water must travel will determine the size of the pump you need.

plants

1 astilbe, page 126

2 hosta, page 127

3 daylily, page 126

4 laevigate iris, page 112

5 goldenrod, page 127

6 water lily, pages 120–125

7 water hyacinth, page 110

8 variegated sweet flag, page 108

runnel

unusual accent

A runnel is a small channel through which water flows. It connects two ponds or stands alone as a unique water feature. You can make it as long or short and as high or low as you want. The only limiting factor is the hose length for the recirculating pump. Runnels provide a rather formal look to landscape design. They look good in courtyards, on terraces, and along entry walks. Building a runnel is easiest if you plan for it from the beginning, although you can add it to an existing walkway.

seasonal care

Although the pump will recirculate water, you may need to replenish the water supply occasionally. Unplug the pump in fall in zones where winter temperatures fall below freezing for days at a time.

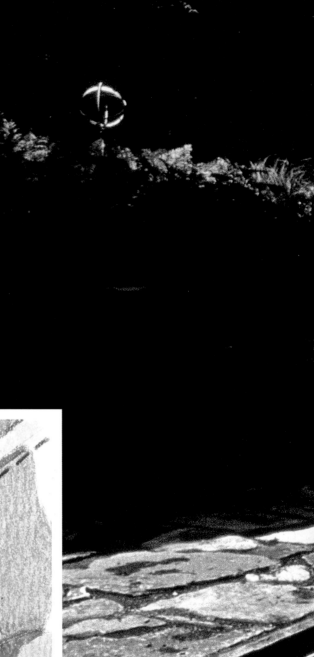

measure stones Use pieces of slate or concrete pavers 1 inch thick by 8 inches wide for the sides and bottom of the runnel. The pieces can be any length. Have the stone cut to fit the exact dimensions you want for the runnel, or build it based on the size of the stones. Have at least eight pieces of stone cut in half lengthwise.

1

dig trench Dig a trench at least 10 inches deep and 12 inches wide. Use a string tied between two stakes to keep the line straight. Add 2 inches of fine gravel to the bottom of the trench.

2

lay stones Lay stones flat on the gravel to form the bottom of the runnel. Apply masonry epoxy between all joints. Use a rubber mallet to tap the stones into place; check that each stone is level. To make the sides, start with a half-piece of stone so the joints of the bottom pieces don't overlap with those of the side pieces. Set the stones on edge, flush with the outside edge of the bottom piece. Cap one end with a half-piece. Build a 16-inch square return box for the pump at the other end.

3

install pump Leave a ½-inch gap between two of the edging stones for the pump cord. Once all stone is in place, use silicone caulk to seal joints that will be under water. Place the pump in the return box and plug it in. Depending on the size of the pump, you may want to attach a return line (a hose for the water to run in) to the pump. Placed at the far end of the runnel, it will move the water the entire length of the feature.

4

freestanding fountain

zones	time	skill
3–11	1 day	easy

you will need

- container–30" or larger in diameter
- pump-and-fountain
- premixed quick-dry cement
- liquid water sealant
- bricks
- outlet with ground fault circuit interrupter

splashing water

One of the simplest water features you can make is a fountain in a container. Use any large pot. Terra-cotta is particularly handsome. If the container does not have a drainage hole in the bottom, drill one (using a masonry bit) or drape the pump's electrical cord over the rim. Disguise the cord by guiding a few stems of one of the surrounding plants along the rim.

Set the freestanding fountain in a garden bed or border that has an electrical outlet nearby; using an extension cord is not recommended.

If you think you will have a problem with mosquitoes, add a few small goldfish, which will eat the larvae. The number of fish you can use—probably not more than two or three—will depend on the diameter and depth of the container.

companion plants

a impatiens
b polka-dot plant

1 Set a submersible pump in the bottom of the container. Using a pot that is at least 30 inches in diameter makes a splash and requires less water refilling than a smaller pot. Pull the pump electrical cord through the drainage hole of the pot.

2 Pull out enough cord to be able to connect it to the outlet–don't plug it in–and leave sufficient slack to raise the pump in the pot. Close the drainage hole with pre-mixed, quick-drying cement. Let the cement dry thoroughly; follow directions on the package.

3 Seal the inside of the pot– whether it is terra-cotta, wood, or some other porous material–with a liquid water sealant that is labeled for use on wood. Let the sealant dry completely.

4 Elevate the pump in the center of the container: Place it on bricks to bring it within a few inches below where the water's surface will be. Fill the pot with water and connect the pump to the GFCI outlet. Be sure the water level does not dip below the pump.

crossing water: stepping-stones

zones	time	skill
4–11	4–5 days	experienced

you will need

- line level, stakes and twine
- nonskid pavers, at least 2" thick × 18" wide
- carpet scraps
- 24"×24" concrete blocks
- 24"×24" capstones (if necessary)
- premixed mortar
- tarp

stepping-stones

Easier maintenance and increased viewing pleasure are the practical and aesthetic reasons for installing stepping-stones. No matter the reason, remember two things for safety: Use stones with a rough surface, so they will not be slippery when wet, and securely fasten the stones to a solid base.

It is easier to install stepping-stones in a pond without water than a filled one. Plan for and construct them as you build the pond; otherwise, drain the pond first.

step placement Be aware of **1** changes in levels on the bottom of the pond and any challenges they may pose. For safety and aesthetics, it is important that you have a level surface on which to walk.

water surface When you have an **2** idea of approximately where you want the stones, drive a stake on either side of an imaginary line passing through the center of where the steps will be. Run twine between the stakes and use a line level to adjust the twine so it is even with where the surface of the water will be.

spacing Lay the pavers on a driveway **3** following the configuration laid out above, and position them so you can walk across them comfortably. Sketch the layout on paper, marking all dimensions.

foundation Place a scrap of carpet **4** where each stepping-stone will be. With the sketch as a guide, put the large concrete blocks on their sides on top of the carpet; stack them until they are ½ inch below the string. (The half-inch allows for the mortar that will be between each of the concrete blocks and the pavers.) You may need to use narrower capstones to get the exact height. Put the pavers in place.

building Mix several batches of mortar. **5** Take apart the piers; then reassemble them using ½ inch of mortar between any blocks all the way up to and including the stepping-stones. Allow the mortar to set for 3 days. Cover everything with a tarp if it rains. Refill the pond.

water gardens | **77**

crossing water: bridge

for one section you will need

Four 6-foot 2×4s treated for underwater use as posts

Two 2-foot 2×4 crosspieces

Two 8-foot 2×8 planks

2 bags concrete mix

8 stainless steel or plated ⅜"×3" lag screws and washers

10 plated 2½" flat head wood screws

wood bridge

The bridge is made of a series of post-and-beam assemblies with planks fastened on top.

This pond is two feet deep, so each assembly requires six-foot full-dimensioned 2×4s to accommodate the three-foot-deep post hole, the pond depth and one foot above the surface. If your pond is deeper or shallower, adjust the length of the 2×4s accordingly. The posts must be treated with creosote or an equivalent water sealant so they won't rot underwater.

plan The concrete must be poured **1**
in dry soil. Ideally you build the bridge
before you fill the pond. Otherwise, drain the
pond and let the soil dry. Plan the zig-zag
course the bridge will take.

dig Using a posthole digger, dig two 3-foot **2**
deep holes, about 18" apart. Since the planks are
treated 2x8s (actually measuring 1½"x7¼"), the
posts will be set about 17" apart to allow some
spacing between and on either side of the planks.

install posts Pour 2" of dry concrete **3**
mix in each hole. Use the post to tamp it down.
Spray a small amount of water (about 1 cup) in
each hole (don't overdo this). Using stakes and
scrap lumber, brace the posts plumb and square
with each other. Pour more dry mix in the holes, a
bit at the time, tamping as you go. Install two more
posts 5 feet away. You may want to install all the
posts at this time. Subsoil moisture will eventually
set the concrete so you don't have to wait to
proceed.

lay bridge Cut the 2x4s into 24-inch **4**
lengths. Pre-drill and screw them to the posts so
the tops of the crosspieces are about 4 inches
above the water. At each connection, use two
⅜"x3" stainless steel or plated lag screws, and
washers. When two crosspieces are in place, lay
down two 8-foot 2x8 planks, overhanging equally
at each end. Pre-drill and, using 2½" flathead
stainless or plated wood screws, fasten the planks
to the crosspieces. Before installing the next
crosspieces, measure up 1½" to accommodate the
overlap of the planks from the next assembly.
Again, screw down through planks at the overlap.
When all planks are installed, cut off post tops (if
necessary) to about 6" above planks.

still water: birdbath

zones	time	skill
4–11	1 hour	easy

you will need

- hoe or shovel
- rubber gloves
- safety glasses
- dust mask
- spray bottle and water
- 3 gallons premixed concrete
- peat moss
- crushed, colored, recycled glass; stone specimens
- plastic sheet

for songbirds

This special handmade birdbath belongs nestled in a flower bed, where admirers will be surprised that it was so easy to make. You don't need a fancy mold to fashion the 18- to 20-inch basin. You can even use a cardboard box instead of the ground, as long as the box is at least 4 inches wider than the basin width. Fill it 10 inches deep with soil; then scoop a basin shape in the soil.

1 create the mold Dig and shape a hole in the ground (or in a soil-filled cardboard box) to use as a mold. Sprinkle the shape with water and pack the soil firmly. Tamp a flat area in the center so the finished basin will sit securely on a flat base.

2 mix concrete and peat Wear gloves and mask. Mix 3 gallons of premixed concrete with 2 to 3 cups of peat moss in a wheelbarrow. Add about 2 gallons of water and mix with a hoe to make a stiff batter. If it is too thin, add more concrete; if too thick to hold together, add water.

3 form the basin Work quickly—concrete starts to set in minutes. Shovel the wet mix into the mold; pat it into place. Conform it to the basin shape; scoop concrete from the center of the basin to the outside rim. Pat smooth. Spritz with water to keep concrete moist.

4 decorate Sprinkle crushed glass on the wet mix; gently press into place. Press in other decorative pieces such as stones. Cover basin with a plastic sheet to cure for 3–7 days. Uncover; remove it from the ground. Age a month before filling with water.

still water

mirror images
right: When you fill a pond or even a small basin or birdbath with clear water, you gain a different perspective. Without plants to obscure the surface, the water shimmers with reflections of fountains and flowers on sunny days. Under cloudy skies, the water becomes a steel-gray opaque expanse.

double duty
right: Make an inviting spot for birds and have a garden ornament at the same time. Find a large flat stone with natural depressions in it or an unusual object such as this column support, right, and tuck it into a border among herbs, perennials, or shrubs. It becomes an instant artful birdbath.

left: A snowcapped birdbath may add interest to a landscape, but you can keep the water from icing over by hooking up a submersible heater.

formal reflection

above: Turn a rectangular (or square) pool into the focal point of a garden by surrounding it with one type of plant (gray-leaved lamb's-ears here) and directing visitors to it with a bluestone path. The water reflects the lamb's-ears, the cherub sitting on the edge, and the leafy canopy.

wall-hung oasis

above: To provide the safest watering hole, raise your birdbath off the ground to prevent predators, such as cats, from threatening the visitors. A hanging birdbath brings the songsters closer to you if you put it on a stair or deck support.

water gardens | **83**

the basics

ecosystem: the life of a pond

a natural microcosm

Your pond is a small ecosystem, so it must find a balance to be healthy and look good. The right combination of plants, fish, snails, and bacteria (present in the water and soil) will result in a balance between sun and shade, oxygen- and carbon dioxide–producers, and food producers and users. The system depends on you to get it off to a good start. A few guidelines for stocking your pond:

- Dechlorinate the water (let it sit for several weeks or you can buy kits to perform the task) and test its pH before putting in any plant material or fish. (The pH should be close to neutral, 7.0.)
- Don't overcrowd the pond with plants or fish; too many of either will promote algae growth and plant and fish diseases.
- Leave at least one-third of the water's surface clear of plants so that sunlight can reach submerged plants and fish.
- Wait 1 to 2 weeks after setting in plants to add fish to the pond.
- While the various parts of the ecosystem are getting in sync, expect algae growth for about 6 weeks after you have stocked the pond. This is normal and will resolve itself.

selecting plants

Of course, most people build a pond so they can enjoy the beauty of water lilies and lotuses. But in addition to their beauty, these plants shade the water, helping to reduce algae growth and providing shelter for fish, both from the sun and from occasional predators.

a pond ecosystem

right: Water lilies cover about 70 percent of this garden; arrowhead and dwarf cattail inhabit the shallower areas. Submerged plants help oxygenate the water.

bog garden

Plants suitable for bog gardens include cardinal flower, cattails, cinnamon fern, pitcher plant, marsh marigold, and Japanese iris. They all prefer consistently moist soil.

Floating plants also provide shade, and use small amounts of nutrients that would otherwise feed algae. The little leaves and flowers present a lovely counterpart to the larger lilies and lotuses in the pond. In very small ponds, you might want to use a floater, such as water snowflake, to take the place of larger water lilies.

Submerged plants (oxygenators) absorb carbon dioxide and release oxygen. Fish use the oxygen and reverse the process. Submerged plants compete with algae for nutrients and light; they provide hiding places and egg-laying sites for fish.

Marginal plants are often used as a vertical backdrop for the pond. Plant them in pots and set them on the pond shelves, or plant them directly in the soil on the outer edge of the pond, where they can use some of the nutrients in the water as well as the soil. The majority of plants in a bog garden are marginals, along with edging plants, which love moisture but do not need to be planted directly in water.

ecosystem: planting

1   **prepare** Water lilies require at least a 5-gallon container that is wider than it is deep–about 17 inches × 9 inches. One with mesh sides allows the roots to breathe underwater without letting the soil escape. If the holes are large, as in this basket, line the container with burlap or landscape cloth. Black or dark green containers are the least noticeable in a pond.

Hardy water lilies are usually sold bare-root or dormant, while tropicals are sold as small, potted plants. When you get the plant, rinse it and remove brown, limp roots. Healthy roots are white. Trim the root system to fit the container. Keep roots moist until you plant. You can plant hardy lilies from spring to mid-July. Wait to plant tropical lilies until the air and water temperatures remain about 70 degrees F.

2   **fill** Fill the container half way with garden topsoil. Avoid potting mixes, which are too light.. Add fertilizer tabs, if you want. Create a shallow well in the soil. Extend it to one side if you plant a hardy water lily; keep the well centered for a tropical water lily.

3   **plant** Water the soil thoroughly. Place a tropical water lily in the center of the container, spreading the roots around the plant.

Position a hardy water lily so the end of the rhizome rests against the side of the container, and the growing tip pokes out of the soil at a 45-degree angle. The growing tip should face the opposite side of the container.

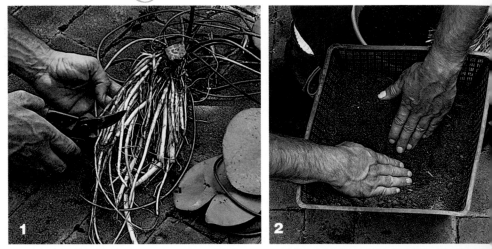

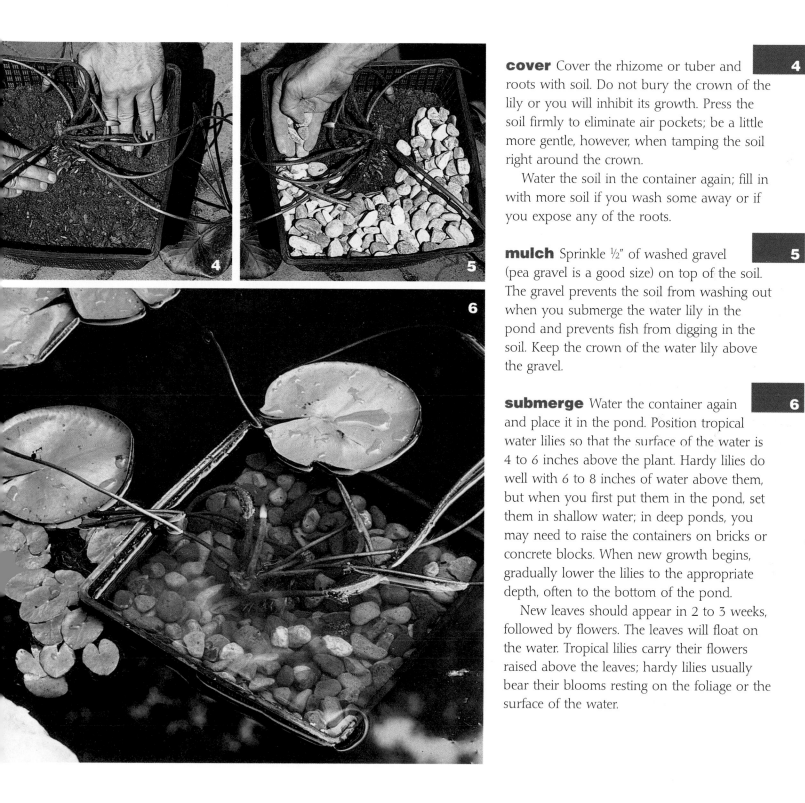

cover Cover the rhizome or tuber and roots with soil. Do not bury the crown of the lily or you will inhibit its growth. Press the soil firmly to eliminate air pockets; be a little more gentle, however, when tamping the soil right around the crown.

Water the soil in the container again; fill in with more soil if you wash some away or if you expose any of the roots.

mulch Sprinkle ½" of washed gravel (pea gravel is a good size) on top of the soil. The gravel prevents the soil from washing out when you submerge the water lily in the pond and prevents fish from digging in the soil. Keep the crown of the water lily above the gravel.

submerge Water the container again and place it in the pond. Position tropical water lilies so that the surface of the water is 4 to 6 inches above the plant. Hardy lilies do well with 6 to 8 inches of water above them, but when you first put them in the pond, set them in shallow water; in deep ponds, you may need to raise the containers on bricks or concrete blocks. When new growth begins, gradually lower the lilies to the appropriate depth, often to the bottom of the pond.

New leaves should appear in 2 to 3 weeks, followed by flowers. The leaves will float on the water. Tropical lilies carry their flowers raised above the leaves; hardy lilies usually bear their blooms resting on the foliage or the surface of the water.

turtles

right: These slow-moving creatures will live in a pond if they have a means of egress. They eat plants and small fish.

fish

below: Select fish to fit the size of your pond. Allow one fish for every 2–3 square feet of surface area. Goldfish are suitable for small ponds, koi for large ones.

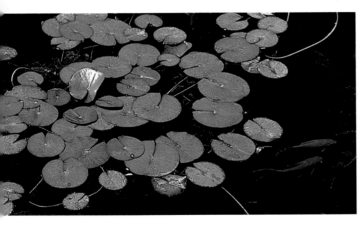

squirrels

right: These nutty creatures will stop for a drink at a pond or birdbath. They will do no harm, even if they bury some of their acorns in the soft, moist soil at the pond's edge. Unlike raccoons, squirrels do not eat fish; they prefer nuts, seeds, and berries.

herons

left: Beautiful as they are to behold on the wing or standing by water, herons can be a threat to pond fish. If herons have begun visiting your new ecosystem and pilfering fish, try covering the pond with netting until the birds tire of their unsuccessful pursuit and move on.

dragonflies

top: Skimming over the surface of the water, dragonflies and their relatives, damselflies, catch their dinners in the air. Mosquitoes are a favorite meal.

frogs

above: Living in the water—and sunning on lily pads—frogs snatch bugs from the air. Although they do occasionally nibble on aquatic foliage, their benefits outweigh any small holes they snack on mosquitoes.

planning & design

planning and siting

The first steps in building a water garden are deciding what kind you want, what your property can accommodate, and where you will put it. Take a good look at your landscape to visualize where the water garden should be; you probably will want to see it from the house as well as from various locations in the yard. The pond itself can be formal or informal, a simple container or a large lined pool, with or without splashing water from a fountain. As you plan, remember a few practical suggestions, such as siting it in as much sun as possible, locating it away from low spots in the yard, and having a water source and GFCI (ground fault circuit interrupt) electrical outlet nearby.

designing

Formal ponds are usually geometric—square, rectangular, or circular. They often have brick or concrete edgings. Informal ponds are free-form, made with either a preformed or a flexible liner, and have rough-cut rocks or flagstones, with undulating groundcovers creeping over the surrounding stones. For the safety of any fish you will include, the edging should overhang the pond to prevent predators easily picking out a free meal.

safety considerations

Before you dig, check with utility companies for the location of all utility lines. Check local building and zoning codes for requirements—such as permits and fencing—as well as restrictions. If you have young children or toddlers, the pond will undoubtedly fascinate them. To keep them safe, make sure the area is securely fenced so they cannot accidentally fall into the pond.

size

above: **Tuck a small water garden in a flower bed for a charming surprise, such as this natural-looking pond surrounded by mossy rocks and accented with whimsical sculpture.**

siting

left: Survey your yard and options before putting shovel to soil. Take into account the hours of sunlight the site receives, the contours of the land, soil composition, and the proximity to electric lines. Avoid a site that does not get at least 6 to 8 hours of sun, that is hilly, rocky, or has utility lines running through it.

design

left: Blend the overall design of your water garden with the surrounding landscape, a technique employed in this pond-and-stream combination. Plantings along the edge repeat plantings elsewhere in the yard. The wooden bridge over the stream matches the fence material. The stream, running parallel to the gravel walk, disappears under the covering of trees and shrubs at the rear—plantings that help camouflage the source of the water.

water gardens | **93**

underlayment Always use an underlay material when building a pond with a flexible liner. Set the underlayment, usually polypropylene/polyester, between the ground and the liner. Cover the sides as well as the bottom of the hole. For more protection, add a layer of old carpet padding, newspapers, or sand on top.

preformed pond liners Made of high-density polyethylene, preformed pond liners come in rectangular and free-form shapes in various widths and lengths. They have built-in ledges and areas for aquatic plants, are relatively small, and do not need any underlayment. They are very easy to install.

flexible liner If you prefer to custom-design your pond, or you want a fairly large water garden, use a flexible EPDM rubber or PVC liner. An EPDM liner is more durable and resistant to temperature extremes, while a PVC liner is lighter, more flexible, and easier to work with. You can trim flexible liners to any size you need. Patching kits are available if you need to repair your flexible (or preformed) pond liner.

mechanicals

modular filter A pump filter extends the life of the pump and keeps the fountain nozzle attached to it free of debris. It doesn't matter if the pond is small or large. Many modular filters are expandable, and they easily disassemble for cleaning and sponge replacement. Available kits include filters along with pumps and fountain nozzles.

pond filter The bio-elements inside pond filters promote good bacteria that remove harmful ammonia and nitrites from your pond, resulting in clean, clear water. Underwater and exterior filters are available. Kits usually have a diverter valve and extension tubes so you can attach the filter to a waterfall, if you want.

skimmer Keeping the surface of a small pond clear of debris is easy with a mechanical pond skimmer or a handheld skimmer.

A large pond pump has a skimmer that catches surface debris in a mesh bag, which is removed and emptied. Exterior versions of skimmers are available that are suitable for large ponds.

enchanting

left: Flower fairies and garden sprites are never out of style. They are delicate-looking sculptures that add a graceful, ephemeral touch to a water garden. Depending on its pose, set one on a rocky ledge above a waterfall or stream, propped up on bricks near a planting of water lilies, or among plants at the edge of the pond.

unusual

below left:: A giant heron, made of macrame over wire frame and BX electrical cable legs, surveys its pond. Before you make or purchase and place a one-of-a-kind sculpture, think carefully about its overall effect on the pond.

recycled

below: Reuse throw-away containers in the garden. Ada Hoffman used wine bottles to stabilize the retaining wall that surrounds one of her many ponds. The bottles imitate the holding ability of rocks. Flowering plants around them become colorful parts of the sculptural design.

ornaments

nostalgic

right: Old boots become delightful accents for a garden or pond. Fill them with water and a tiny plant or two. You can make a humorous or nostalgic statement with many old items that have lost their original usefulness: iron kettles, leaky watering cans, stacks of mossy terra-cotta pots, rusted tools, even wooden ladders with missing rungs. No spruce-up is required before you place them near your pond.

contemplative

left: A large stone with a water-filled depression sets the scene as a small space for thoughtful, quiet contemplation. Add another stone for accent, cluster a few plants nearby, or even float a flower in the water. Although you may consider it a contemplative water garden, you'll likely find birds coming to bathe.

amusing

left: Water gardening isn't always a serious business. Witness this playful decoration near the far edge of this pond: a mannequin head wearing a soft-brimmed hat. Especially if you have young children or teenagers, lighten your idea of what is appropriate for your pond, and invite them in on the decision making.

surprising

below left: Let your imagination loose in your gardens. Unexpected accents, such as these handsome ceramic fish swimming through a mixed border, announce your appreciation of the unusual. They also intrigue visitors with a hint of what may lie around the bend in the path—your water garden.

serene

above: Water pouring from this Oriental-style feature can be softly pleasing or loud enough to mask undesirable sounds. For the biggest splash, set the bamboo pole so it pours into a large vessel, at least 2 feet in diameter. A small pump recirculates the water after the bamboo pole fills and dumps it.

maintenance & troubleshooting

a **spring clean-up** If you have not put protective screening or netting over the pond (see below), it will have winter debris floating on the surface and lying on the bottom. Remove light objects, such as dead leaves and twigs, with a skimmer.

b **fall cover-up** To avoid the chore of scooping out fallen leaves from the pond, place netting or screening over it in autumn. (Screening has smaller openings and catches finer debris.) To make it easier to remove the screening for dumping, nail it inside a frame made with 2×4s or lumber scraps.

c **remove screen** If you have fish, leave the screening in place through winter to provide some protection for them when the surface foliage is gone. Remove it in early spring before plants start to grow.

d **drain pond** Every three to five years, you will want to drain your pond to remove the sludge that inevitably collects on the bottom.

Place all plants (potted, floating, and submerged) in buckets in the shade; wrap moist newspapers around them. Use your pump to drain the water, or siphon it off with a hose. When the water level has dropped sufficiently, move the fish to large net-covered buckets (so the fish can't jump out) filled with pond water. Shovel out the nutrient-rich sludge and use it as mulch on your plants or put it on the compost pile.

do regular chores Be as observant **e** about the plants in your pond as you are with your other gardens. Remove dying or spent flowers, discolored or dead leaves, and broken stems. Keep the water level consistent, topping it off as necessary to replace water lost to evaporation during hot summer weather.

remove excesses Wade into a **f** shallow (less than 2' deep) pond to do regular maintenance–removing any unwanted plants and cutting off dead foliage and flowers–during the growing season.

In fall, do a thorough clean-up of plants. Cut back potted plants and set them on the bottom of the pond. Disconnect and lower the pump to the bottom of the pond.

Have a de-icer ready to plug in as freezing weather approaches.

ready the pond in spring Replace **g** pond and pump filters. If you had the pump recirculating at a reduced volume during winter, clean pump screen, outlet, and tubing.

Bring potted plants up to their proper level under the water's surface; replace any that have died. Repot plants that have outgrown their containers.

Check the health of your fish; begin feeding them when the water temperature reaches 50 degrees.

Don't worry about algae bloom which that occurs naturally in spring as the water temperature in the pond rises. It should go away within a month if you have fish in the water.

h   **skim off scum** Scum on the water or on plant leaves is not pleasant to look at and is not good for plants or fish. It usually appears only in ponds fed by a natural stream, and the cause may be pollution upstream. One solution might be to filter the water as it enters your pond; another would be to close off the stream's entrance to the pond until you can alleviate the problem.

Wash the scum off the plant leaves by swishing them in the water, and skim it out of the pond as often as necessary.

i   **remove stains** Stains on stones or rocks, caused by iron deposits or hard water, can be unsightly around a pond. To remove such stains, take the stone out of the pond, or away from the rim if it is an edging stone, and bleach it. You cannot treat it with bleach while it is in position because any bleach that gets in the water will harm both fish and plants.

Mix a solution of ¼ cup bleach in 2 quarts water. Don't clean the stone on or near a deck or other wooden structure –the bleach will stain it.

j   **build a barrier** If deer, raccoons, opossums, or other creatures are a threat to your pond's fish and plants, put up an unobtrusive low-voltage electric fence.

Space the wires 1 to 2 feet apart on poles high enough to deter the pests.

You may be able to remove the fencing after a period of time, unless the wildlife is very hungry.

fishy friends In addition to being colorful additions to a pond, fish are good neighbors. They eat mosquitoes and their larvae, aphids, and caterpillars. They dine lightly on some algae. They exhale carbon dioxide, which plants need. Keep an eye on your fish to make sure they are healthy. If they are sluggish, it may be due to a variety of problems such as a lack of oxygen in the water from too many plants covering the surface or too few submerged oxygenators. Add a pump and fountain to help aerate the water. Another problem is an overly high pH–fish prefer a pH close to neutral.

summer algae A certain amount of algae in a pond is normal. Too much, however, spoils the look of the pond and can harm fish and submerged plants. Warm weather or an ecological imbalance promotes algae growth. There are a few solutions: Decrease the number of fish (you may have more than the pond can accommodate); if you feed the fish (optional) stop for a while so they will eat more algae; increase the number of submerged oxygenators.

invasive plants Unfortunately, a few of the most popular plants for water gardens can become real pests, spreading invasively, especially if they escape from your pond. Some states (particularly in warmer zones) ban or restrict certain plants; check with your Cooperative Extension office before you include them in your pond. Among the most rampant are duckweed, *left*, water hyacinth, water willow, horsetail, and water mint.

recommended
plants

common and botanical names

Common name	Botanical name
american swamp lily	*Saururus cernuus*
arrowhead	*Sagittaria* spp.
astilbe	*Astilbe* spp.
bigleaf ligularia	*Ligularia dentata* 'Desdemona'
blue flag	*Iris versicolor*
bog lily (swamp lily)	*Crinum americanum*
bull rush	*Scirpus* sp. *(Isolepis cernua)*
burr reed	*Sparganium erectum*
butterbur	*Petasites japonicus*
caladium	*Caladium* hybrids
calla lily	*Zantedeschia aethiopica*
canna	*Canna* 'Pretoria'
cape pondweed	*Aponogeton distachyos*
cardinal flower	*Lobelia cardinalis*
cattail	*Typha* spp.
chinese water chestnut	*Eleocharis dulcis*
chameleon plant	*Houttuynia cordata* 'Chamaeleon'
cinnamon fern	*Osmunda cinnamomea*
clivia	*Clivia* spp.
common yellow water lily	*Nuphar polysephala*
corkscrew rush	*Juncus effusus* 'Spiralis'
cranberry	*Vaccinium macrocarpum*
creeping jenny	*Lysimachia nummularia*
daylily	*Hemerocallis* spp. and cvs.
duck potato	*Sagittaria latifolia*
duckweed	*Lemna minor*
dwarf papyrus	*Cyperus haspan*
elephant's ear	*Colocasia esculenta*
fairy moss	*Azolla* spp.
floating fern	*Azolla* spp.; *Ceratopteris pteridoides*
four-leaf water clover	*Marsilea mutica*
giant rhubarb	*Gunnera manicata*
giant water lily	*Victoria cruziana*
goldenrod	*Solidago* spp. and cvs.
great blue cardinal flower	*Lobelia siphilitica*
green taro	*Colocasia esculenta*
gunnera	*Gunnera manicata*
hardy water canna	*Thalia dealbata*
horsetail	*Equisetum hyemale*
hosta	*Hosta* spp.
impatiens	*Impatiens* cvs.
indian cup	*Sarracenia purpurea*
indian pond lily	*Nuphar polysephala*
japanese iris	*Iris ensata*

japanese pittosporum	*Pittosporum tobira*
japanese primrose	*Primula japonica*
kaffir lily	*Clivia* spp.
laevigate iris	*Iris laevigata* 'Albopurpurea'
leucothoe	*Leucothoe* spp.
lizard's tail	*Saururus cernuus*
lotus	*Nelumbo* spp.
maranta	*Maranta bicolor*
marsh marigold	*Caltha palustris*
meadow rue	*Thalictrum delavayi*
moneywort	*Lysimachia nummularia*
papyrus	*Cyperus papyrus*
parrot feather	*Myriophyllum aquaticum*
pickerel rush	*Pontederia cordata*
pitcher plant	*Sarracenia* spp.
pondweed	*Potamogeton* spp.
purple taro	*Colocasia* 'Jet Black Wonder'
rush	*Juncus* spp.
sedge	*Carex* spp.
siberian iris	*Iris siberica*
skunk cabbage	*Lysichiton* spp.
spike rush	*Eleocharis montevidensis*
swamp lily	*Crinum americanum*
swamp milkweed	*Asclepias incarnata*
sweet flag	*Acorus calamus*
umbrella palm	*Cyperus alternifolius*
umbrella plant	*Darmera peltata*
wapato	*Sagittaria latifolia*
watercress	*Nasturtium officinale*
water fern	*Ceratopteris pteridoides*
water fringe	*Nymphoides peltata*
water hawthorn	*Aponogeton distachyos*
water hyacinth	*Eichornia crassipes*
water lettuce	*Pistia stratiotes*
water lily	*Nymphaea* spp. and cvs.
water mint	*Mentha aquatica* 'Crispa'
water pennywort	*Hydrocotyle ranunculoides*
water poppy	*Hydrocleys nymphoides*
water snowflake	*Nymphoides indica variegata*
white trumpet	*Sarracenia leucophylla*
wild rice	*Zizania aquatica*
yellow flag	*Iris pseudacorus*
yellow floating heart	*Nymphoides peltata*
zebra rush	*Schoenoplectus lacustris* 'Zebrinus'

Acorus calamus 'Variegatus'
variegated sweet flag
Marginal plant
Perennial; 2'–4' tall
Flowers greenish; fragrant
Blooms spring to summer
Sun or light shade
Set plant 5"–6" under water surface
Zones 4–10

Vivid green, lance-shape leaves striped with creamy white; reminiscent of iris. (Foliage has a citrusy fragrance when crushed.) Good vertical accent. Non-variegated type available.

Aponogeton distachyos
water hawthorn (cape pondweed)
Submerged oxygenator
Perennial; 8" tall
Flowers white; fragrant
Blooms spring and fall
Sun or light shade
Set plant 8"–24" under water surface
Zones 9–11

Surface leaves are straplike, may be evergreen in warm climates. Free-flowering. A decorative plant for any pond. May be invasive; remove spent blooms to prevent seed formation.

Asclepias incarnata
swamp milkweed
Edge plant
Perennial; 3' tall
Flowers rosy pink; fragrant
Blooms summer
Sun
Zones 3–11

Wonderful thick-stemmed, branching plant for the edge of a pond, especially one with a natural look. Very free-flowering. Attracts butterflies as does its relative, *A. tuberosa*.

water garden plants

Azolla spp.
floating fern (fairy moss)
Floater
Perennial, 3"–4" long
No flowers
Sun or light shade
Zones 8–11

The lacy pea-green leaves turn dark red or purple in the cooler weather of fall. Most species will not survive frost, but *Azolla caroliniana* survives by means of submerged fragments. Can be aggressive, covering the surface of a pond, and is best for containers.

Caladium hybrids
caladium
Edge or marginal plant
Perennial, 18" tall
No flowers; bicolor, multicolor leaves
Shade or partial sun
Set plant 2"–3" under water surface
Zones 10–11

Tuberous-rooted plants with arrowhead-shape leaves in amazing color combinations, including silver-white, crimson-pink-white, red-green, and gray-white-dark green-maroon. Prefers constantly moist soil. May be potted and submerged. Dig up and store tubers indoors for winter.

Caltha palustris
marsh marigold
Edge or marginal plant
Perennial; 18" tall
Flowers yellow
Blooms spring
Light shade
Set plant 6" under water surface
Zones 4–10

Cabbage-like leaves. Plant clumps along the edge of a pond or in it. Bright yellow flowers are 2 inches across, held in clusters. There are double-flowered and white-flowered forms. Dies to the ground in summer; tuck it where other plants will cover the space.

Canna 'Pretoria'
canna
Marginal or edge plant
Perennial; 4'–6' tall
Flowers deep orange
Blooms summer
Sun or light shade
Set plant 6" under water surface
Zones 7–11

Very decorative plants that look best in medium or large ponds. In colder zones, dig up tubers and store indoors for winter.

Colocasia 'Jet Black Wonder'
[syn. 'Black Magic']
purple taro
Marginal plant
Perennial; 3'–4' tall
No flowers
Sun or light shade
Set plant 6"–8" under water surface
Zones 8–11

Stunning plum-purple foliage and stems. Grows well in very moist soil at the edge of a pond or in the center. Treat as an annual in colder zones or bring indoors for winter.

Ceratopteris pteridoides
water fern (floating fern)
Floater
Perennial; 12"–18" long
No flowers
Sun or light shade
Set plant 3"–12" under water surface
Zones 10–11

New plants form on the triangular leaves. Sterile fronds float or are partially submerged; fertile fronds usually rise erectly from the middle of the sterile fronds. Spreads rapidly and can be a nuisance. Float the plants on the surface or pot them.

Crinum americanum
bog lily (swamp lily)
Edge or marginal plant
Perennial; 18"–24" tall
Flowers white or pink; sweetly fragrant
Blooms midsummer
Sun
Set plant 2"–6" under water surface
Zones 9–11

The straplike leaves and spidery blooms create a spectacular accent. Plant along the edge of the pond or near the perimeter. In colder areas bring the plant indoors for winter.

Colocasia esculenta
elephant's ear (green taro)
Marginal or edge plant
Perennial; 3'–7' tall
No flowers
Sun or light shade
Set plant up to 12" under water surface
Zones 9–11

The large, velvety leaves, which can grow up to 3 feet long, add a tropical look. In colder climates, bring the potted plant indoors or dig up the tuber and store it indoors for winter.

Cyperus alternifolius
umbrella palm
Marginal plant
Perennial; 5'–8' tall
Flowers tan
Blooms summer
Sun or shade
Set plant 5"–6" under water surface
Zones 9–11

One of the mainstays of a water garden. Adds graceful height and movement, even in a slight breeze. Very easy to grow. Overwinter indoors in colder zones.

Cyperus haspan (C. profiler)
dwarf papyrus
Marginal plant
Perennial; 12"–24" tall
Flowers tan
Blooms summer
Sun or shade
Set plant no more than 2" under water surface
Zones 9–11

Delightful plant for even the smallest pond or container garden. In colder zones, bring the potted plant indoors for winter and keep the soil constantly moist.

Cyperus papyrus
papyrus
Marginal plant
Perennial; 6'–10' tall
Flowers greenish brown
Blooms summer
Sun or light shade
Set plant 6" under water surface
Zones 9–11

Striking plant for a larger water garden. Pendulous leaflike bracts. Ancient source of paper. Cannot withstand frost and is difficult to bring indoors because of its size.

Darmera peltata
umbrella plant
Edge plant
Perennial; 3' tall
Flowers white to bright pink
Blooms spring
Sun
Zones 6–11

The only plant in this genus, native to northwestern California and southwestern Oregon. Flowers appear before the foliage. A dramatic plant for a pond's edge. 'Nana' is a smaller cultivar, growing about 12 inches tall.

Eichhornia crassipes
water hyacinth
Floater
Perennial; 5"–6" tall
Flowers violet blue with yellow blotch
Blooms summer
Sun
Zones 9–11

Easy to grow as an annual in colder areas. Flower resembles a hyacinth, held above the leaves on strong stems. Very invasive: Never dispose of excess plants in sewers or streams. May not be sold across state lines.

Eleocharis dulcis [E. tuberosa]
chinese water chestnut
Marginal plant
Perennial; 1'–3' tall
Flowers green
Blooms late spring–late summer
Sun
Zones 9–11

Graceful stems. Tubers are used in many Chinese dishes. Good in container or tub gardens as well as any size pond. (See page 25 for directions on growing in a container.) Do not confuse with *Trapa natans*, European water chestnut, which is invasive and prohibited in the United States.

Eleocharis montevidensis
spike rush
Marginal plant
Perennial; 12" tall
Flowers light brown
Blooms late spring–late summer
Sun or light shade
Set plant 2"–3" under water surface
Zones 6–11

A favorite food of wildlife. Tiny flowers are followed by fruiting spikes in autumn. The narrow, quill-shape leaves are very attractive near the edge of small and medium-size ponds. Spreads quickly but is not invasive.

Equisetum hyemale
horsetail
Marginal plant
Perennial; 18"–48" tall
Flowers are spiky cones
Blooms summer and fall
Sun or light shade
Set plant 6" under water surface
Zones 3–11

Good vertical accent. Horsetail can be invasive, so plant it in pots. Dwarf horsetail grows to 8 inches; crown should be 1 inch below water surface.

Gunnera manicata
gunnera (giant rhubarb)
Edge plant
Perennial; 6'–13' tall
Flowers green tinged red
Blooms summer
Sun or light shade
Zones 8–11

Best suited for the banks of very large ponds because its huge crinkled leaves can grow 6 feet wide or more. Clump forming. The plant to grow for a tropical, architectural effect, especially where it can be reflected in the water. Grows best in mud.

Houttuynia cordata 'Chamaeleon'
chameleon plant
Marginal or edge plant
Perennial; 10"–12" tall
Flowers white
Blooms late spring–early summer
Sun or light shade
Set plant 1"–3" under water surface
Zones 3–8

Decorative in or out of the pond. Best used in containers for added color.

Hydrocleys nymphoides
water poppy
Floater or marginal plant
Perennial; 3"–4" tall
Flowers yellow with purple stamens
Blooms summer
Sun
Zones 8–10

Easy to raise as an annual in colder areas. Will grow as a free-floating plant or rooted in a pot and set in shallow (4"–6") water. Can be invasive; not allowed in California.

Hydrocotyle ranunculoides
water pennywort
Marginal, floating-leaved plant
Perennial; 3" tall
Flowers greenish white
Blooms spring–summer
Sun or light shade
Set plant 2" under water surface
Zones 5–11

Bright green, scalloped leaves. Will root at nodes anywhere they touch soil. *H. vulgaris* and *H. verticillata* make good, fairly fast-growing cover plants.

Iris ensata [*I. kaempferi*] 'Velvety Queen'
japanese iris
Edge or marginal plant
Perennial; 3' tall
Flowers violet-and-white
Blooms summer
Sun
Set plant 1" under water surface
Zones 6–9

Gorgeous plants for the pond's edge or in shallow water. Many cultivars to choose from with striking flower colors: yellow, white, purple, pink, blue, and crimson.

Iris laevigata 'Albopurpurea'
laevigate iris
Marginal plant
Perennial; 2'–3' tall
Flowers purple and white
Blooms early summer
Sun or light shade
Set plant 2"–4" under water surface
Zones 4–9

Beautiful plant adds color and height. Some selections have variegated leaves. Mass in large ponds; use as accents in smaller ones. After the flowers fade, the foliage remains attractive.

Iris siberica
Siberian iris
Edge plant
Perennial; 2'–3' tall
Flowers lilac, blue, purple, white
Blooms late spring–early summer
Sun
Zones 4–9

Will grow in shallow, 1-inch deep water, as well as in moist, boggy soil along the edge of a pond. Narrow, green leaves. Good for any size water garden.

Iris pseudacorus
yellow flag
Marginal plant
Perennial; 3'–5' tall
Flowers clear yellow, occasionally white
Blooms early to mid-spring
Sun or light shade
Set plant 6"–9" under water surface
Zones 4–9

The first blooms of spring. Mass plants for most spectacular effect. The sword-shape, blue–green foliage is attractive all season. Will survive in up to 18 inches of water.

Iris versicolor
blue flag
Marginal plant
Perennial; 3' tall
Flowers soft blue-purple, pink, magenta
Blooms early summer
Sun or light shade
Set plant 6" under water surface
Zones 4–9

Native to the eastern United States. Graceful, narrow foliage. 'Kermesina' is a good selection for smaller ponds. 'Rosea' has pink flowers.

Iris pseudacorus 'Variegata'
variegated yellow flag
Marginal plant
Perennial; 4'–5' tall
Flowers yellow
Blooms early summer–midsummer
Sun or light shade
Set plant 6"–9" under water surface
Zones 4–9

The light yellow striping on the leaves fades they mature in summer. Excellent for any size pond–even a small one..

Juncus effusus 'Spiralis'
corkscrew rush
Marginal plant
Perennial; 30"–48" tall
Flowers brown, insignificant
Blooms summer
Sun
Set plant 5" under water surface
Zones 4–9

Less invasive than the species soft rush (*Juncus effusus*). The twisting stems add unusual interest to any size pond; plant height makes it good for smaller ponds.

plants

Juncus subnodulosus
blunt-flowered rush
Marginal plant
Perennial; 3'–3½' tall
Flowers greenish white
Blooms summer
Sun
Set plant 3"–5" under water surface
Zones 6–10

Leaves are narrow and sword-shape. Shorter than corkscrew rush; good for any size pond. More noticeable flower heads add to its effect along the perimeter of the pond.

Lobelia cardinalis
cardinal flower
Edge or marginal plant
Perennial; 2'–3' tall
Flowers scarlet
Blooms mid- to late summer
Sun
Set plant 3"–4" under water surface
Zones 3–9

Stunning planted in groups around any size pond. Cut flower stalks to the ground after blooms fade to promote a second flowering.

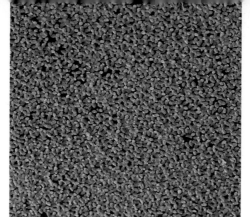

Lemna minor
duckweed
Floater
Perennial; ⅓"-wide leaves
Insignificant flowers
Sun or light shade
Zones 4–11

Incredibly easy to grow, duckweed is a minute plant that quickly covers a wide area. It is said to be the smallest and simplest of all flowering plants. The plants are all frond–no leaves or stems–that may be tinged red. A favorite food of fish and waterfowl. Confine to a small pond or a container. Can be invasive.

Lobelia siphilitica
great blue cardinal flower
Edge or marginal plant
Perennial; 2'–2½' tall
Flowers blue, white-tipped
Blooms midsummer
Light shade or sun
Set plant 3"–4" under water surface
Zones 5–9

Very free-flowering. Lance-shape leaves are lightly covered with fine hairs. The white-flowered form, 'Alba', is good for brightening shady areas.

Ligularia dentata 'Desdemona'
bigleaf ligularia
Edge plant
Perennial; 3'–4' tall
Flowers yellow-orange
Blooms midsummer
Light shade or sun
Zones 4–9

Striking large purple leaves that fade to a metallic green. Good companion to *Gunnera* and *Colocasia*. Prefers moist but not soggy soil. Avoid planting in full sun in warmer zones.

Lysichiton americanum
western skunk cabbage
(yellow skunk cabbage)
Edge plant
Perennial; 3'–4' tall
Flowers bright yellow; unpleasantly fragrant
Blooms spring
Sun or light shade
Zones 6–9

The unique flowers do not last long–the bold foliage provides interest until the first fall frost. Can survive as a marginal plant if no more than 1 to 2 inches of water covers the roots.

113

Lysichiton camtschatcensis
white skunk cabbage
Edge plant
Perennial; 3' tall
Flowers white; unpleasantly fragrant
Blooms spring
Sun or light shade
Zones 6–9

From Asia, the plant has the same growing requirements as yellow skunk cabbage. Its leaves are more compact. The flowers appear slightly later than those of the yellow skunk cabbage.

plants

Marsilea mutica
four–leaf water clover
Edge or marginal plant
Perennial; 3"-long leaves
No flowers
Sun, light shade, or shade
Set plant 3"–12" under water surface
Zones 6–11

Related to ferns, water clover looks like a four-leaf clover. Its small, lightly patterned leaves are a good contrast to pads of water lilies. It can become invasive when planted in an earth-bottom pond or in soil around the edge; best grown in pots.

Lysimachia nummularia
creeping jenny (moneywort)
Submerged or edge plant
Perennial; 3'-long shoots
Flowers yellow
Blooms early summer
Sun or shade
Zones 3–8

Very fast-spreading oxygenator. Delightful solitary flowers. Equally at home carpeting a bank or planted in up to 2 inches in water, creeping over the pond's surface. It may be too invasive for smaller ponds.

Mentha aquatica 'Crispa'
water mint
Marginal or edge plant
Perennial; 6" tall
Flowers lilac; very fragrant
Blooms summer
Sun or light shade
Set plant 2"–4" under water surface
Zones 6–11

Like its cousins, the garden mints, water mint spreads rapidly. Plant it in a container or in the ground around a pond to soften the edge (if you don't mind its prolific growth). In moist soil, water mint will grow to 3 feet tall; in water, it will spread with a height of about 6 inches.

Maranta bicolor
maranta
Edge plant
Perennial; 10"–14" tall
Flowers white
Blooms summer
Light shade
Zones 10-11

Most often treated as an indoor plant where it is not hardy outdoors, maranta can be an effective contrast outdoors to other pond-edging plants. Its brown-spotted pale green leaves are purple beneath.

Myriophyllum aquaticum
parrot feather
Submerged oxygenator or marginal plant
Perennial; 6" tall
No flowers
Sun or light shade
Set plant 3"–12" under water surface
Zones 6–10

Great for containers or any size pond. Delicate-looking, bright green foliage. Useful as an oxygenator, completely submerged, and as a decorative marginal plant. Stems can grow up to 5 feet long. (Not to be confused with *Myriophyllum spicatum*, Eurasian water milfoil, which is banned in the United States.)

Nasturtium officinale
watercress
Marginal or edge plant
Perennial; 12" tall
Flowers white
Blooms spring–early summer
Sun
Zones 6–9

Attractive, glossy, deep green leaves are edible. Likes moving, rather than still water. Plants root where any stem node touches soil. Stems and leaves will float as well as creep.

Nelumbo lutea (N. pentapetala)
American lotus
Perennial; 6"–10" flowers, 1'–1½'-wide leaves
Flowers pale yellow; slightly fragrant
Blooms summer
Sun
Set plant 6"–8" under water surface
Zones 4–11

A magnificent plant. Flowers may be held on stems 2–5 feet above the water. All lotuses are day-blooming; most flowers last for 3 days. All have decorative seed pods. Place in pond so container is fully submerged. Appropriate for any size water garden.

Nelumbo nucifera (N. speciosa)
sacred lotus
Perennial, 12" flowers, 2'–3'-wide leaves
Flowers pink fading to cream; very fragrant
Blooms summer
Sun
Set plant 6"–12" under water surface
Zones 4–11

The sacred lotus of Buddhism. Hybrids are gorgeous plants for the larger water garden. Single and double blooms; shades of white edged pink, deep pink, red, yellow. Dwarf varieties and cultivars are good in tubs.

Nuphar polysephala
Indian pond lily
(common yellow water lily)
Submerged oxygenator; floating-leaved plant
Perennial; 6"–18" leaves; 4"–5"-wide flowers
Flowers yellow; fragrant
Blooms late spring–late summer
Sun
Zones 4–11

Plant and care for this as you would water lilies, which it resembles. Prefers slightly alkaline water. Provides shade and protection for fish.

Nymphoides indica variegata
water snowflake
Submerged oxygenator; floating-leaved plant
Perennial; 5"-wide leaves
Flowers white, stained yellow at center
Blooms summer
Sun or light shade
Set plant 3"–18" under water surface
Zones 8–11

Easy to grow as an annual in colder areas. Has attractive heart-shaped, mottled leaves. Very invasive; planting in container and removing excess plants may keep it under control.

Nymphoides peltata
water fringe (yellow floating heart)
Submerged oxygenator; floating-leaved plant
Perennial; 2"-wide leaves
Flowers bright yellow
Blooms summer
Sun or light shade
Zones 6–10

Often used in small ponds and containers as a substitute for water lilies. The foliage has burgundy variegations. Provides quick cover in newly planted ponds, but is invasive; plant it in a pot to control its spread.

Petasites japonicus
butterbur
Edge plant
Perennial; 3'–4' tall
Flowers greenish white; fragrant
Blooms spring
Sun
Zones 5–11

Huge leaves, 3–4 feet high and wide, make a dramatic statement by a large pond. Flowers appear before the leaves. A variegated form has leaves spotted yellow to cream. Reminiscent of *Gunnera*. May be invasive.

plants

Potamogeton spp.
pondweed
Submerged oxygenator
Perennial; 10'–13' spread
Flowers pale pink
Blooms early summer
Sun
Zones 5–9

Curled pondweed, *Potamogeton crispus*, is a noninvasive plant with reddish bronze leaves; it looks like seaweed. Fennel pondweed, *P. pectinatus*, has narrow green leaves with tubers that provide food for waterfowl.

Pistia stratiotes
water lettuce
Floater
Perennial; 4"–10" tall
Flowers white, inconspicuous
Blooms summer
Sun or light shade
Zones 9–11

Beautiful long roots, changing color from white to purple, indigo, and black, hang down in the water. Good for containers. Easy to grow as an annual. Can be invasive where it is winter-hardy; banned in many states.

Primula japonica
japanese primrose
Edge plant
Perennial; 2' tall
Flowers pink, white, crimson
Blooms late spring
Sun or shade
Zones 5–8

One of the best massed plants to lend a natural woodland aspect to the water garden. A candelabra-type produces layers of flowers on multiple stems. There are many cultivars: 'Fuji' and 'Miller's Crimson' have quantities of crimson flowers; 'Postford White' has a yellow eye; 'Valley Red' is bright red. Divide plants every 3 years.

Pontederia cordata
pickerel rush
Marginal plant
Perennial; 2'–3' tall
Flowers blue
Blooms summer to early fall
Sun or light shade
Set plant 5"–12" under water surface
Zones 3–9

Lovely plant for any size pond. Eye-catching blue flower spikes (unusual color for water plants). Attracts bees. Edible fruit. Remove spent blooms to encourage flower production.

Sagittaria graminea
arrowhead
Marginal plant and submerged oxygenator
Perennial; 1'–4' tall
Flowers green and white
Blooms summer
Sun
Zones 6–10

Submerged and surface leaves. Shape of the surface leaves on most species gives the plant its common name. Excellent for vertical accent in pond. Prefers still water. .

Sagittaria latifolia
duck potato (wapato)
Marginal plant and submerged oxygenator
Perennial; 2' tall
Flowers green and white
Blooms summer
Sun
Set plant 3"–6" under water surface
Zones 4–11

Very easy to grow. Decorative accent. Because tubers are a food source for waterfowl as well as humans, you may need to cage the pots to keep them for yourself.

Sagittaria sagittifolia [syn. *S. japonica*]
'Flore Pleno'
double–flowering arrowhead
Marginal plant
Perennial; 3'–4' tall
Flowers white, double
Blooms summer
Sun or light shade
Set plant up to 6" under water surface
Zones 7–11

Showy with whorls of double globular flowers and decidedly arrow-shape leaves. Plant in very moist soil or in water. Harder to establish than the single-flowered species.

Sarracenia flava
yellow pitcher plant
Edge plant
Perennial; 4' tall
Flowers yellow
Blooms spring
Sun or light shade
Zones 7–11

Carnivorous plant from southeastern United States. Do not collect from the wild. Pitcher is yellow-green, often reddish or maroon at tips and base. Likes very moist, mucky soil.

Sarracenia leucophylla
white trumpet
Edge plant
Perennial; 3½' tall
Flowers reddish purple
Blooms spring
Sun
Zones 8–11

The pitcher is green below, white with green, maroon, or red veins above. Carnivorous plant native to central and southeastern United States. Do not collect from the wild.

Sarracenia purpurea
pitcher plant (Indian cup)
Edge plant
Perennial; 12" tall
Flowers dark red or yellow
Blooms spring
Sun
Zones 3–8

Carnivorous plant with evergreen leaves. Its pitcher is green variegated with purple or red veins or entirely green. Native to eastern North America. Do not collect from the wild.

Saururus cernuus
lizard's tail (American swamp lily)
Marginal plant
Perennial; 12"–24" tall
Flowers white; fragrant
Blooms summer
Sun or light shade
Set plant 6" under water surface
Zones 4–9

Native to southeastern United States. Fruits that follow the flower spikes give the plant its common name. Bright green foliage. Plant near side of the pond.

117

Schoenoplectus lacustris 'Zebrinus'
[Scirpus lacustris ssp. *tabernaemontani]*
zebra rush
Marginal plant
Perennial; 3'–6' tall
No flowers
Sun, tolerates light shade
Zones 4–9

A short plant for shallow water, it has horizontal cream bands along the stems. The coloration adds interest, especially if plants are set against a dark background, where they seem to glow.

plants

Scirpus spp. *[Isolepis cernua]*
bull rush
Marginal plant
Perennial; 6'–10' tall
Flowers brownish
Blooms late summer
Sun, tolerates light shade
Set plant 2"–12" under water surface
Zones 5–9

Grasslike stems form vertical accents at pond's edge. Grow in groups and in containers to curtail its invasive tendencies. Species have fluffy or spiked flowers at the tips.

Sparganium erectum
burr reed
Marginal plant
Perennial; 3'–4' tall
Flowers greenish white
Blooms late summer
Sun
Set plant about 18" under water surface
Zones 6–10

The sword-like leaves form a good background in a large pond. Waterfowl eat the seeds. All burr reeds can be invasive; *S. erectum* is prohibited in Florida.

Thalia dealbata
hardy water canna
Marginal plant
Perennial; 2'–6' tall
Flowers violet
Blooms summer
Sun or light shade
Set plant 12"–24" under water surface
Zones 6–11

Although from subtropical America, hardy water canna can usually survive winter if planted deep in the water. Canna-like, blue-green leaves and flower panicles are lovely, tropical accents.

Thalictrum delavayi [T. dipterocarpum]
meadow rue
Edging plant
Perennial; 5' tall
Flowers lilac or white
Blooms summer
Sun
Zones 7–9

The dainty leaves and airy panicles of these flowers are excellent contrasts to the bold foliage of most marginal and edging water garden plants. Stake these plants so they do not flop over in the wind. Flower sprays can reach up to 2 feet long. Among the variations are 'Album' and 'Hewitt's Double'.

Typha angustifolia
narrow–leaved cattail
Marginal plant
Perennial; 4'–5' tall
Flowers brown
Blooms late summer
Sun or light shade
Set plant 2"–5" under water surface
Zones 3–11

With their grasslike leaves, cattails create attractive vertical interest and movement in a pond. They can be invasive, so plant in containers. Attracts waterfowl.

Typha latifolia
cattail

Marginal plant
Perennial; 7'–9' tall
Flowers dark brown
Blooms late summer
Sun or light shade
Zones 3–11

A good choice for larger ponds if you want a tall accent. Straplike leaves. Very invasive and almost impossible to control if its rhizomes escape the container. 'Variegata', with creamy variegation, is shorter and less invasive.

Victoria cruziana
giant water lily

Night-blooming; 4'–6' spread each leaf
Flowers white changing to pink, then purple-red; fragrant the first night they open
Blooms summer
Sun
Zones 5–11

An amazing curiosity. Requires a pond at least 20 feet in diameter. 'Longwood Hybrid', a cross between this species and *Victoria amazonica*, is larger, hardier, and produces more flowers.

Typha minima
dwarf cattail

Marginal plant
Perennial; 12"–18" tall
Flowers chocolate-brown
Blooms late summer
Sun or light shade
Set plant 2" under water surface
Zones 3–11

Perfect for the smallest water gardens and for container gardens. Very narrow, grasslike leaves. Flower spikes are round instead of the usual oblong.

Zantedeschia aethiopica
calla lily

Marginal plant
Perennial; 2'–3' tall
Flowers white; fragrant
Blooms summer
Sun
Zones 8–11

May survive in colder zones if submerged in 12 inches of water. Arrow-shape foliage is striking. Use along the perimeter of the pond or raised in the center as a focal point. 'Crowborough' is smaller (to 2 feet) and hardier; 'Little Gem' is dwarf (to 1 foot).

Vaccinium macrocarpum
cranberry

Edge plant
Perennial; 1'–6' tall
Flowers white or pink; reddish fruit
Blooms spring
Light shade
Zones 2–10

Its interesting growth habit makes it suitable for a wild garden that edges a pond. Leaves turn bright red in fall. Fruit is edible and attractive to wildlife as well as humans.

Zizania aquatica
wild rice

Marginal plant
Annual; 8'–9' tall
Flowers creamy white
Blooms summer
Sun or shade
Zones 9–11

Deep green, scaly leaves. Makes an excellent sculptural, vertical accent, either potted near the margin of the pond in shallow water or in the ground along the edge. Attracts wildlife. *Zizania latifolia* is smaller, growing to 4 feet; it is a hardy perennial in Zones 9–11.

stars of the water garden

Undoubtedly the main reason people become enamored of ponds is the water lilies that fill them with color, fragrance, and form. Water lilies are one of the most beautiful of the floating-leaved plants, for foliage as well as flowers. Their beauty is difficult to resist, but resist growing them to the exclusion of other plants. For balance–the ecology of the pond as well as the overall design–put in companion plants: floaters and floating-leaf plants, submerged plants, marginal and edging plants.

design considerations

To design with water lilies, use accompanying plants to harmonize and contrast with the beautiful colors of the flowers and the color variations of the leaves. Select plants that add vertical dimension, contrasting textures, and non-competitive fragrance.

cultural factors

Most water lilies need at least 6 hours of sun daily. They prefer still water; keep them away from fountains and waterfalls.

Set potted water lilies on the bottom of the pond.

Fertilize monthly, using tablets formulated for use in water gardens; push the tablets into the soil in the pot.

Groom the plants periodically: Remove spent blooms and yellowed leaves.

At season's end, cut back the stems and pads of hardy water lilies; move plants to the deepest part of the pond. Discard tropical water lilies or remove the tubers that form on the roots and store tubers in water in a cool, dark location until spring.

Nymphaea gigantea var. *alba*
gigantea water lily
Tropical water lily
Day-blooming; 7'–8' spread
Flowers pale blue violet, white, or pink; lightly fragrant
Blooms summer
Sun
Zones 10–11

The large flowers may be blue, white (var. *alba*), or pink (var. *violacea*). Striking blooms, held 1 foot above the water. Their wide spread requires a large pond. Blue variety may be sold under the name 'Blue Gigantea'.

Nymphaea odorata 'Sulphurea'
hardy water lily
Perennial; 3'–4' spread
Flowers yellow; sweetly fragrant
Blooms summer
Sun
Zones 3–11

Blooms open from late morning to mid-afternoon. A very old water lily hybrid, dating from the late 1870s; still popular and very easy to grow. Good for medium and large ponds.

water lilies

Nymphaea stellata
blue lotus of India
Tropical water lily
Day-blooming; 4½'–5' spread
Flowers pale blue, barely fragrant
Blooms summer
Sun
Zones 10–11

Mistakenly called the blue lotus of India, because it is not a lotus at all, *Nymphaea stellata* (syn. *N. nouchali*) grows as happily in container gardens as it does in small and large ponds. Blooms are held about 1 foot above the water. It is a treasure, and it may be difficult to find.

Nymphaea x *helvola*
miniature water lily
Perennial; 1½' spread
Flowers canary yellow; lightly fragrant
Blooms summer
Sun
Zones 3–11

The tiny 1½- to 2-inch blooms and purple-mottled leaves are exquisite in containers and small ponds. Blooms open in early afternoon. Also known as 'Yellow Pygmy', it is a cross between *Nymphaea. tetragona* and *N. mexicana*.

Nymphaea 'Albert Greenberg'
tropical water lily
Perennial; 6½' spread
Day-blooming; blend of pink, yellow, and
    orange; fragrant flowers
Blooms summer to late summer or early fall
Sun or partial sun
Zones 10–11

Attractive purple-blotched foliage. The 6- to
7-inch cup-shape blooms remain open into
late evening. Very easy to grow. Good for
containers as well as medium to large ponds.

Nymphaea 'Attraction'
hardy water lily
Perennial; 6' spread
Flowers deep garnet red, sometimes flecked
    white; only slightly fragrant
Blooms late spring–summer
Sun or light shade
Zones 3–11

Mature flowers are 7 inches across; one of the
largest red hardy lilies. Young blooms are
pinkish white, small, and cuplike, deepening in
color as they mature and take on a star shape.

Nymphaea 'Andriana'
hardy water lily
Perennial; 3'–4' spread
Flowers reddish orange and yellow; slightly
    fragrant
Blooms summer
Sun
Zones 3–11

Large blooms and leaves; produces many
flowers. Petals change color as they mature–
the inner petals from reddish orange to rusty
orange, the outer petals from pale yellow to
peach-yellow. Leaves are blotched reddish
brown. Excellent in any size pond.

Nymphaea 'Bob Tricket'
tropical water lily
Perennial, day-blooming; 6'–6½' spread
Flowers light blue with gold anthers tipped in
    blue; very fragrant
Blooms summer
Sun
Zones 10–11

Large leaves are red underneath and have
undulating margins. Huge flowers about
14 inches across. Easy to grow. Good for
medium and larger ponds.

the wonders of water lilies
Water lilies are wonderfully diverse. There
are hardy and tropical lilies; in the
latter group there are day-bloomers and
night-bloomers.

hardy water lilies
As a group, hardy water lilies are quite
tough. Hardy lilies usually display their
flowers and leaves on the water's surface.
They produce blooms in shades of white,
pink, red, orange, and yellow–almost
every color except blue. The changeables
open one color and subtly change
through various shades as they mature
over 3–4 days. Most hardies are only
slightly fragrant. There are small and
miniature cultivars as well as very large
ones, in terms of flower and leaf size and
overall spread. Hardies are day-blooming:
The flowers open in mid- to late morning
and usually close by late afternoon.

tropical water lilies
In many areas of the world, gardeners
treat tropical water lilies as annuals
because they will not survive cold or
freezing temperatures. They are very easy
to grow and inexpensive enough that you
need not worry about replacing them
every year. If you live in zones 10 to 11,
tropicals will be perennial for you.
Tropicals usually display their flowers
on stems that are 1 foot tall or taller.
Flowers are larger than those of the
hardy water lilies are, are intensely
fragrant, and come in every color,
including various hues of blue.

Day-blooming water lilies open in the
morning and close in the afternoon.
Night-blooming water lilies open
at dusk and remain open until
sunrise–or later.

water gardens | **121**

Nymphaea 'Charles de Meurville'
hardy water lily
Perennial; 3'–7' spread
Flowers red, tipped with pale pink or white; fragrant
Blooms summer
Sun
Zones 3–11

Flowers are 6–7 inches across and are held above the foliage, more like those of a tropical water lily's flowers. Leaves are very large (8 inches across).

water lilies

Nymphaea 'Charles Thomas'
tropical water lily
Day-blooming; 4'–5' spread
Flowers periwinkle blue; sweetly fragrant spring–summer
Sun or light shade
Zones 10–11

Star-shape blooms above purple-blotched leaves. Excellent for containers as well as for small and large ponds. One of the best blue-flowered tropical water lilies. Will take more cold than many blue tropicals.

Nymphaea 'Comanche'
hardy water lily
Perennial; 4'–5' spread
Flowers apricot changing to copper red; fragrant
Blooms late spring–summer
Sun
Zones 3–11

Foliage opens purple and matures to dark green. It is the showiest of the orange-blend water lilies and is susceptible to crown rot. Does well in all climates.

Nymphaea 'Darwin'
hardy water lily
Perennial; 4'–6' spread
Flowers soft pink, double; slightly fragrant
Blooms summer–fall
Sun
Zones 3–11

A very popular water lily, it is easy to grow and flowers prolifically with double, peony-type 5½– to 6-inch blooms. Inner petals start out white, turn pink as they mature. Formerly known as 'Hollandia'.

Nymphaea 'Dauben'
tropical water lily
Day-blooming; 3'–4' spread
Flowers light blue with lavender tips, fading to creamy white; very fragrant
Blooms late spring–summer
Sun or light shade
Zones 10–11

A lovely, easy-to-grow water lily that is perfect for the first-time water gardener. Its compact size makes it suitable for containers as well as small ponds. Blooms remain open longer than most day-bloomers. Withstands more cold than most tropicals. (Known as 'Daubeniana' in Europe and elsewhere.)

Nymphaea 'Emily Grant Hutchings'
tropical water lily
Night-blooming; 6'–7' spread
Flowers deep rose-pink; slightly fragrant
Blooms late spring–summer
Sun or light shade
Zones 10–11

Very large flowers (10" across) held above bronze-tinged foliage. Produces blooms and new plants on short runners very freely. Good choice for beginning gardeners. Excellent for any size pond. (Restrict its growth by potting it in a smaller container.)

Nymphaea 'Georgia Peach'
hardy water lily
Perennial; 6'–8' spread
Flowers yellow and pink blend; fragrant
Blooms summer–late summer
Sun
Zones 3–11

A relatively new cultivar. Delicate-looking plant with lightly mottled leaves. It is very free-flowering. Good for both medium and large ponds.

Nymphaea 'H. C. Haarstick'
tropical water lily
Night-blooming; 6'–12' spread
Flowers deep red; fragrant
Blooms summer–fall
Sun
Zones 10–11

Developed at the Missouri Botanical Garden in St. Louis, this is one of the first night-blooming water lilies. Large, showy, rather flat flowers have a tinge of purple at the base of some of the petals. Leaves are reddish brown on top, purple underneath; they can reach 16 inches across.

Nymphaea 'Joey Tomocik'
hardy water lily
Perennial; 6'–12' spread
Flowers golden yellow; spicy fragrance
Blooms late spring–late summer
Sun or light shade
Zones 3–11

Very easy to grow. The 4- to 5-inch flowers appear constantly over a long season. The light green leaves are flecked with brown.

Nymphaea 'Louise'
hardy water lily
Perennial; 4'–5' spread
Flowers red with white-tipped light pink
  sepals; sweetly fragrant
Blooms late spring–late summer
Sun
Zones 3–11

The green leaves have a bronze tint when young. Will produce more flowers if it is planted in a large container. Excellent for any size pond.

Nymphaea 'Madame Ganna Walska'
tropical water lily
Day-blooming; 4'–12' spread
Flowers violet-pink; fragrant
Blooms summer
Sun or light shade
Zones 10–11

An easy and constant bloomer, flowering with as little as 3 hours of sun daily. Leaves are strongly mottled with maroon. Named for the Polish opera singer Madame Walska, who created Lotusland in Santa Barbara, California.

Nymphaea 'Maroon Beauty'
tropical water lily
Night-blooming; 6'–12' spread
Flowers deep red with purple undertones;
  fragrant
Blooms late spring–summer
Sun
Zones 10–11

Stamens are tipped with red. Flowers are about 10 to 12 inches across and held high above the foliage. Leaves are reddish brown when young. It is best for larger ponds because of the potential spread of its leaves.

123

Nymphaea 'Mrs. Edward Whitaker'
tropical water lily
Day-blooming; 6'–7' spread
Flowers light blue; fragrant
Blooms summer
Sun
Zones 10–11

Bred by George Pring and introduced in 1917, this is still one of the best water lilies for medium ponds. The flowers can reach 12 inches in diameter.

Nymphaea 'Pink Beauty' ('Luciana')
hardy water lily
Perennial; 4'–5' spread
Flowers salmon-pink; slightly fragrant
Blooms late spring–fall
Sun or light shade
Zones 3–11

Great plant for beginning gardeners: easy to grow, reliable bloomer, long flowering season. Good for any size pond, especially smaller ones. Formerly known as 'Fabiola'.

Nymphaea 'Pink Star'
tropical water lily
Day-blooming; 10'–12' spread
Flowers pink; fragrant
Blooms summer
Sun
Zones 10–11

A chance seedling of 'Red Star', from the early 1900s. Typical of the star lilies, it withstands cold better than most tropicals. Best in a very large water garden because of its spread.

water lilies

Nymphaea 'Red Flare'
tropical water lily
Night-blooming; 5'–7' spread
Flowers deep red; slightly fragrant
Blooms summer
Sun
Zones 10–11

Dramatic water lily with large blooms, up to 10 inches across, held 12 inches above the striking maroon leaves. Older leaves have wavy, serrated edges. Good for any size pond.

Nymphaea 'Rhonda Kay'
tropical water lily
Day-blooming; 6'–9' spread
Flowers violet blue; sweetly fragrant
Blooms summer
Sun
Zones 10–11

A relatively new introduction, fewer than 20 years in cultivation. Flowers prolifically. Blooms are held 12 to 18 inches above the foliage–it is usually the tallest flower in a pond. Does well in medium to large ponds.

Nymphaea 'Rose Arey Hybrid'
hardy water lily
Perennial; 4'–5' spread
Flowers medium pink; sweetly fragrant
Blooms early spring–fall
Sun
Zones 3–11

Its parent, 'Rose Arey', has been called one of the most beautiful lilies known. New purple leaves turn green as they mature. Begins to bloom earlier in spring than most other water lilies, and the blooms open earlier in the morning. A choice selection for a medium or large pond.

Nymphaea 'Shirley Bryne'
tropical water lily
Day-blooming; 3'–4' spread
Flowers cerise; delicately fragrant
Blooms summer
Sun
Zones 10–11

Blooms open from late morning to mid-afternoon. A brilliantly colored flower that adds fragrance to the garden during the daytime. Good for medium and large ponds.

Nymphaea 'Texas Shell Pink'
tropical water lily
Night-blooming; 5'–6' spread
Flowers creamy white with reddish purple
    tips; cinnamonlike fragrance
Blooms late spring–summer
Sun or light shade
Zones 10–11

Attractive shading from white to reddish purple gives the 6- to 8-inch flowers a frosted look. Very dependable for prolific blooming and easy care.

Nymphaea 'St. Louis Gold'
tropical water lily
Day-blooming; 4'–6' spread
Flowers deep yellow; slightly fragrant
Blooms late spring–late summer
Sun
Zones 10–11

Good for any size pond, including container water gardens and small pools. Flowers open late and remain open late. Very free-flowering. Olive green leaves are attractive, with small purple blotches on new leaves.

Nymphaea 'Virginalis'
hardy water lily
Perennial; 3'–4' spread
Flowers white; slightly fragrant
Blooms late spring–fall
Sun
Zones 3–11

Very easy to grow and produces an abundance of flowers over a long season. Green leaves have a bronze cast to them when they are new. One of the most reliable white-flowered hardy water lilies.

Nymphaea 'Sumptuosa'
hardy water lily
Perennial; 4'–5' spread
Flowers deep pink to carmine inner petals;
    white to pale pink outer petals; slightly
    fragrant
Blooms summer–fall
Sun
Zones 3–8

Flowers lightly flecked with white. Grows well in the Pacific Northwest. Often sold as 'Masaniello', a similar bicolor.

Nymphaea 'Virginia'
hardy water lily
Perennial, 5'–6' spread
Flowers pale yellow inner petals, white outer
    petals; slightly fragrant
Blooms summer to fall
Sun
Zones 3–11

The large and showy flowers are most fragrant on the first day they open. Some think of it as a white version of 'Sulphurea Grandiflora', a classic from the late 1880s. Good for medium and large ponds.

125

the surrounding landscape

When you plant a pond, consider the area just beyond the perimeter. Blend the water garden with the immediate vicinity as well as with your other garden beds. The most important consideration for selecting plants for that purpose is their need for water. Here is the spot for moisture-loving ferns and other perennials and annuals.

Many of these plants also grow well in a rather shady location, especially one with afternoon shade cast by tall, deciduous trees. Even though you will find maintenance and building easier if you site a pond away from trees, you may want a woodland ambience. Plants such as astilbes, ferns, hostas, leucothoe, and impatiens will provide excellent plant material for such a scene.

Agapanthus cvs.
lily-of-the-nile
Perennial; 1'–4' tall
Flowers blue, white
Blooms spring–summer
Sun
Zones 7–11

Beautiful plant with strap-shape leaves adds a tropical look to the edge of the garden. In Zones 3–8, grow it in a pot and bring indoors for winter. Prefers moist, well-drained soil; slightly drier in fall and water. Many cultivars available in various shades of blue or white.

Astilbe cvs.
astilbe (false goat's beard)
Perennial; 18"–40" tall
Flowers pink, rose, purple, white
Blooms early summer
Light shade or partial sun
Zones 5–8

Astilbes are beautiful foliage plants when not in bloom and are excellent foils for hostas and ferns at the shaded edges of a pond. There are many cultivars from which to choose.

companion plants

Carex elata
variegated sedge
Perennial; 1'–2½' tall
Flowers light brown
Blooms summer
Sun
Zones 7–11

Graceful grasslike foliage. Grows well in up to 4 inches of water and along the perimeter of a pond in soil that is constantly very moist. 'Bowles Golden' and 'Aurea' have bright green and golden yellow variegations; 'Variegata' has green and white striped leaves.

Clivia spp. and cvs.
clivia (kaffir lily)
Perennial; 1'–2' tall
Flowers orange, scarlet, yellow (rare)
Blooms winter–spring
Light shade or partial sun
Zones 10–11

Well-known as an indoor plant, it is equally valuable as a stunning tropical accent near a water garden. In Zones 10–11, plant in the ground; in all other areas, plant in pots to bring indoors in late summer/early fall. Keep soil evenly moist in spring and summer, slightly drier in fall and winter. The plant is attractive in or out of bloom.

Hemerocallis spp. and cvs.
daylily
Perennial; 1'–4' tall
Flowers yellow, cream, pink, deep red, every color except blue, many bicolor; some are fragrant
Blooms spring–late summer
Sun or very light shade
Zones 3–9

With such an overwhelming number of cultivars, it is possible to have a lush garden of daylilies alone. Some are repeat-bloomers. A perennial with foliage that looks good all season. Likes moist soil but will survive droughts. Good for stabilizing slopes.

Hosta spp. and cvs.

hosta

Perennial; 12"–48" tall
Flowers lavender, white; some slightly fragrant,
    grown mostly for their foliage
Blooms midsummer
Shade or partial sun
Zones 3–9

Many cultivars available, with broad and
wavy or lance-shape leaves, which may be
green, bluish, or chartreuse, banded, edged, or
streaked with cream or white. Excellent hardy
specimen as well as groundcover plant.

Osmunda cinnamomea

cinnamon fern

Perennial; 20"–30" tall
Shade, light shade, or partial sun
Zones 3–11

The cinnamon-brown color of the fertile
fronds gives this fern its common name.
May grow to 5 feet. Turns tawny gold in
fall. Grows best in constantly moist soil. Royal
fern (*O. regalis*) is also perfect by water, planted
with flag iris and hosta. Other appropriate
ferns include holly fern (*Polystichum munitum*),
Japanese painted fern (*Athyrium niponicum*
'Pictum'), lady fern (*A. filix-femina*), and
maidenhair fern (*Adiantum pedatum*).

Impatiens cvs.

impatiens (busy lizzie)

Annual; 10"–18" tall
Flowers pink, white, coral, red, bicolor
Blooms late spring–early fall
Shade or partial sun

Easy-care plants that will bloom nonstop
if you fertilize them monthly during the
growing season. Plant in moist soil with
good drainage in shade or, in northern
zones, in areas with some morning sun.
Faded blooms usually drop from the plants.
Use impatiens to edge the garden or group
them like nosegays.

Pittosporum tobira

Japanese pittosporum

Shrub or small tree; 8'–10' tall
Flowers white, yellow; sweetly fragrant
Blooms late spring–early summer
Sun or light shade
Zones 8–11

Broad-leaved evergreen. Attractive specimen
plant with leathery leaves; some have gray-
green foliage with white variegations. A good
seaside plant, it will also grow as an indoor
plant in colder regions.

Leucothoe spp. and cvs.

leucothoe

Shrub; 3'–4' tall
Flowers white
Blooms late spring
Light shade
Zones 5–8

Broad-leaved evergreen grown for its foliage,
which may emerge red, turn green or
variegated pink and cream, and mature to
burgundy or bronze in fall. 'Scarletta' and
'Nana' have dwarf growth habits.

Solidago spp. and cvs.

goldenrod

Perennial; 3'–4' tall
Flowers yellow
Blooms late summer
Sun or partial sun
Zones 3–9

Golden yellow panicles of blooms. The species
can run rampant–lovely if your pond is in a
naturalistic setting–but cultivars are more
sedate. 'Golden Dwarf', 'Queenie' (leaves
variegated green and gold), 'Golden Shower',
and 'Crown of Rays' are excellent by water,
especially attractive if planted so they are
reflected on the surface.

127

sources

Water gardening, is so popular that most nurseries, garden centers, and home centers carry supplies, fish, and plants. If you can't find what you want locally, make use of these sources.

Mail–Order Plants, Fish, and Equipment Suppliers

Beckett Corporation (E)
5931 Campus Circle Dr.
Irving, TX 75063-2606
888-BECKETT
www.beckettpumps.com

Burpee (S) free
300 Park Ave.
Warminster, PA 18991-0001
800-487-5530
www.burpee.com

Busse Gardens (P) $3.00
17160 245th Ave.
Big Lake, MN 55309
800-544-3192
www.bussegardens.com

Crystal Palace Perennials (A, E, P) $2.00
P.O. Box 154
St. John, IN 46373
219-374-9419
www.crystalpalaceperennial.com

Girard Nurseries (A, P) free
P.O. Box 428
Geneva, OH 44041-0428
440-466-2881
www.girardnurseries.com

Heronswood Nursery Ltd. (P) $8.00
7530 NE 288th St.
Kingston, WA 98346
360-297-4172
www.heronswood.com

Kurt Bluemel, Inc. (P) $3.00
2740 Greene Ln.
Baldwin, MD 21013-9523
800-248-7584
www.bluemel.com

Lilypons Water Gardens (A, E, F, P) $5.00
P.O. Box 10
Buckeystown, MD 21717-0010
800-879-5459
www.lilypons.com

Niche Gardens (P) $3.00
1111 Dawson Rd.
Chapel Hill, NC 27516
919-967-0078
www.nichegdn.com

Paradise Water Gardens (A, E, F, P) free
14 May St.
Whitman, MA 02382
800-955-0161
www.paradisewatergardens.com

Park Seed Company (S) free
One Parkton Ave.
Greenwood, SC 29647-0001
800-845-3369
www.parkseed.com

Plant Delights Nursery (P)
9241 Sauls Rd.
Raleigh, NC 27603
919-772-4794
www.plantdelights.com

Pond Supplies of America, Inc. (E) free
1204 Deer St.
Yorkville, IL 60560
888-PICK-PSA
www.pondsupplies.com

S. Scherer & Sons (A, E, P) $1.00
104 Waterside Rd.
Northport, NY 11768
516-261-7432
www.netstuff.com/scherer

Slocum Water Gardens (A, E, P) $3.00
1101 Cypress Gardens Blvd.
Winter Haven, FL 33884-1932
941-293-7151
www2.slocumwatergardens.com

Song Sparrow Perennial Farm (P) free
13101 East Rye Rd.
Avalon, WI 53505
800-553-3715
www.songsparrow.com

Thompson & Morgan Inc. (S) free
P.O. Box 1308
Jackson, NJ 08527-0308
800-274-7333
www.thompson-morgan.com

Tranquil Lake Nursery (P) $1.00
45 River St.
Rehoboth, MA 02769-1395
508-252-4002
www.tranquil-lake.com

William Tricker, Inc. (A, E, F, P) $2.00
7125 Tanglewood Dr.
Independence, OH 44131
800-524-3492
www.tricker.com

Van Ness Water Gardens (A, E, F, P) $4.00
2460 N. Euclid Ave.
Upland, CA 91784-1199
www.vnwg.com

Waterford Gardens (A, E, F, P) free
74E Allendale Rd.
Saddle River, NJ 07458
201-327-0721
www.waterfordgardens.com

Water Garden Gems, Inc. (A, E, F) free
3136 Bolton Rd.
Marion, TX 78124-6002
210-659-5841

Plants exclusively from the Internet

www.garden.com
www.landscapeusa.com

climate

Hardiness zones and first and last frost dates are helpful guides. The main thing to remember about using such maps is that they are guides for averages only. Consider many factors in addition to these ranges in order to be successful in growing plants. One consideration is the number of very hot summer days in your region; heat can be as detrimental to plants as cold. Cope with that by setting plants in an exposure that has some protection from midday sun, especially in the Deep South. Another component for success is good soil–for aquatic plants, that means ordinary garden soil. Keep average frost dates in mind when planting annuals and marginally hardy or very tender perennials. If you plant tender plants in the garden too early in spring or leave them there too late in fall, you run the risk of frost destroying them.

USDA hardiness zone map

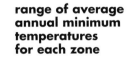

**range of average
annual minimum
temperatures
for each zone**

	Zone 1	Below -50°F
	Zone 2	-50° to -40°
	Zone 3	-40° to -30°
	Zone 4	-30° to -20°
	Zone 5	-20° to -10°
	Zone 6	-10° to 0°
	Zone 7	0° to 10°
	Zone 8	10° to 20°
	Zone 9	20° to 30°
	Zone 10	30° to 40°
	Zone 11	Above 40°

spring frost dates

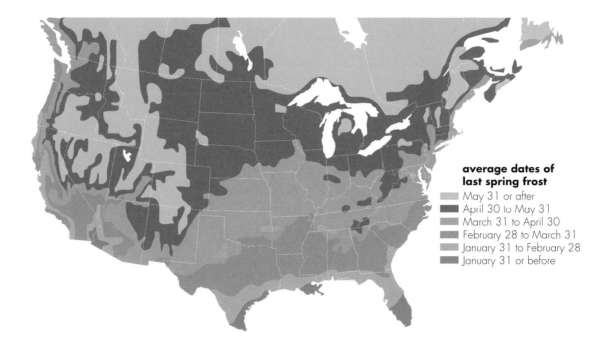

average dates of last spring frost
- May 31 or after
- April 30 to May 31
- March 31 to April 30
- February 28 to March 31
- January 31 to February 28
- January 31 or before

fall frost dates

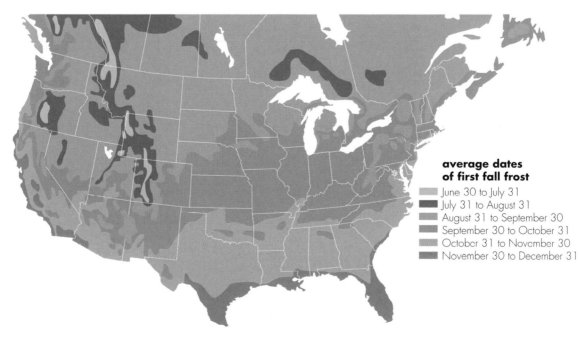

average dates of first fall frost
- June 30 to July 31
- July 31 to August 31
- August 31 to September 30
- September 30 to October 31
- October 31 to November 30
- November 30 to December 31

index

index

index

index

index

photography credits

Ernest Braun:
98 (top right)

C. Colston Burrell:
110 (top right), 114 (top left)

David Cavagnaro:
11 (bottom), 12, 22, 50
(bottom), 59 (top right), 70–71;
84, 85 (bottom), 90 (top left),
91 (left), 91 (top right), 103
(bottom), 104, 108 (top left),
108 (top right), 108 (bottom
left), 109 (top center), 109 (top
right), 109 (bottom left), 110
(bottom left), 111 (top center),
111 (top right), 111 (bottom
left), 111 (bottom center), 111
(bottom right), 112 (top left),
112 (top center), 112 (top
right), 112 (bottom center),
113 (top right), 113 (bottom
left), 113 (bottom center), 114
(top center), 114 (top right),
114 (bottom left), 115 (top
center), 115 (bottom left), 115
(bottom center), 115 (bottom
right), 116 (top left), 116 (top
center), 116 (bottom left), 116
(bottom right), 117 (bottom
center), 117 (bottom right), 118

(top left), 118 (top center), 118 (top right), 118 (bottom left), 118 (bottom center), 118 (bottom right), 119 (top left), 119 (top right), 120 (bottom left), 121 (bottom left), 125 (top left), 125 (bottom center), 127 (top left)

Crandall and Crandall:
44 (top left)

Rosalind Creasy:
8 (top), 24 (center), 25 (top), 25 (top center), 25 (bottom center), 25 (bottom), 83 (bottom), 115 (top left), 119 (bottom right)

Charles Cresson:
55 (top right), 55 (bottom right), 113 (bottom right), 117 (top left), 117 (top center), 117 (top right), 117 (bottom left)

Bill Holt:
103 (top left)

Dency Kane:
9 (top), 9 (bottom), 11 (top), 16–17, 20, 26, 44 (bottom left), 64 (bottom right), 93 (top left), 93 (bottom left), 100 (bottom),106 (bottom left),

109 (bottom center), 116 (bottom center)

Brian E. McCay:
15 (top), 19 (center right), 23 (top), 23 (top center), 23 (bottom center), 23 (bottom)

Charles Mann:
6–7, 29 (right center), 65 (bottom right), 109 (bottom right), 110 (bottom center), 113 (top left), 115 (top right), 119 (top center), 122 (top right), 122 (bottom right)

Anne Meyer:
94–95 (all)

Stephen Pategas:
112 (bottom right), 114 (bottom center), 119 (bottom left)

Roger Sherry:
72–73 (all)

Charles Thomas:
1 (top), 3 (top), 4 (top), 105 (bottom), 120 (top left), 120 (top right), 120 (bottom right), 121 (top right), 121 (bottom right), 122 (top left), 122 (top

center), 122 (bottom left), 122 (bottom center), 123 (top left), 123 (top center), 123 (top right), 123 (bottom left), 123 (bottom center), 123 (bottom right), 124 (top center), 124 (top right), 124 (bottom left), 124 (bottom center), 124 (bottom right), 125 (top center), 125 (top right), 125 (bottom left), 125 (bottom right)

Saba S. Tien:
4, 8 (bottom), 10 (bottom left), 27 (top right), 53 (top right), 54–55 (center), 78–79, 64 (top left), 86 (top right), 96 (top), 97, 99 (top left), 99 (bottom right), 100 (top left), 100 (top right), 100 (center), 101 (top left), 101 (top right), 101 (bottom), 102 (top right), 102 (bottom), 103 (top right), 108 (top center), 108 (bottom center), 108 (bottom right), 110 (top left), 110 (top center), 111 (top left), 113 (top center), 114 (bottom right), 119 (bottom center), 121 (top left), 124 (top left), 126 (top center), 126 (bottom left), 127 (bottom left)

credits

credits

Beckett Corporation:
Pond supplies, mechanicals, ornaments, photographs, fountains

Gardens and gardeners:
BH&G Test Garden, Marie Calliet, Rosalind Creasy, Charles Cresson, Robert Dash, Vincent Desjardin & Jim Dailey, Jeanne Dolan, Donna & Andy Durbridge, Anstace & Larry Esmonde-White, Sandra Gerdes, Ada Hoffman, Marlen Kemmet, Niche Gardens, Old Westbury Gardens, Ellen Penick, Happy & Everett Post, Barbara Pressler, River Farm, S. Scherer & Sons, Ton Stam & David Clem, Valerie Strong,, Saba S. Tien

metric conversions

U.S. Units to Metric Equivalents

to convert from	multiply by	to get
Inches	25.400	Millimetres
Inches	2.540	Centimetres
Feet	30.480	Centimetres
Feet	0.3048	Metres
Yards	0.9144	Metres
Square inches	6.4516	Square centimetres
Square feet	0.0929	Square metres
Square yards	0.8361	Square metres
Acres	0.4047	Hectares
Cubic inches	16.387	Cubic centimetres
Cubic feet	0.0283	Cubic metres
Cubic feet	28.316	Litres
Cubic yards	0.7646	Cubic metres
Cubic yards	764.550	Litres

To convert from degrees Celsius (C) to degrees Fahrenheit (F), multiply by ⁹⁄₅; then add 32.

Metric Units to U.S. Equivalents

to convert from	multiply by	to get
Millimetres	0.0394	Inches
Centimetres	0.3937	Inches
Centimetres	0.0328	Feet
Metres	3.2808	Feet
Metres	1.0936	Yards
Square centimetres	0.1550	Square inches
Square metres	10.764	Square feet
Square metres	1.1960	Square yards
Hectares	2.4711	Acres
Cubic centimetres	0.0610	Cubic inches
Cubic metres	35.315	Cubic feet
Litres	0.0353	Cubic feet
Cubic metres	1.308	Cubic yards
Litres	0.0013	Cubic yards

To convert from degrees Fahrenheit (F) to degrees Celsius (C), first subtract 32; then multiply by ⁵⁄₉.